WHAT PEOPLE ARE SAYING ABOUT RIDICULOUSLY AMAZING SCHOOLS

"*Ridiculously Amazing Schools* is a lively read. I could not put it down. It uses powerful anecdotes to deliver important messages. This book should be in the hands of every educator. We should all be working through the challenges and insights presented in this book. Our schools and educators are the lifeline of our world. Jeff and Tracey have delivered an engaging and accessible framework for transforming the lives of our educators and the students they teach."

Sally J. Zepeda, Ph.D.
Professor of Educational Administration and Policy
University of Georgia

"Jeff and Tracey capture the spirit of reciprocity that exists in education through poignant stories and pragmatic solutions. *Ridiculously Amazing Schools* is a refreshing read that illuminates a transformative path forward free from gimmicks or shortcuts. In doing so, they show us that when we invest in the people around us, we inevitably become better ourselves."

Dr. Brad Gustafson
National Distinguished Principal and Best-Selling Author

"*Ridiculously Amazing Schools* is what has been missing and what has been needed from education professional development literature ... a complete focus on the well-being of our educators. Most education PD books provide practical insight centered around all things students. Jeff and Tracey have stepped outside of that box to provide incredible perspective and real-world examples of why taking care of the educators first will ultimately impact our students in a profound way. Not only are the examples relevant to our schools today, the ideas for cultural changes can be implemented the next day! This first-of-its-kind book definitely hits the mark!!!"

Kirk Jones, Principal
Ayersville Middle School
Defiance, Ohio

"*Ridiculously Amazing Schools* is a brilliant distillation of the experience and understanding of how to build a winning culture in schools that can only be developed from years in the trenches, building one meaningful relationship at a time. The wisdom in this book extends far beyond the walls of education, though—any leader managing a team can benefit from its lessons. I've always believed that the best teachers and coaches are the ones who can take as much important information as possible and distill it down to simple steps and directives. And, if that's the standard, *Ridiculously Amazing Schools* is an invaluable guide for leaders everywhere."

Kyle Porter, Owner
The Hawcreek Dojo
Cumming, Georgia

"Most educational licensure programs prepare students for obstacles with instruction, state/federal laws, and school finances; what they often miss out on is preparing educators for each other. *Ridiculously Amazing Schools* can help fill that void. With the reflection tools as a guide, the lessons and advice shared by Jeff and Tracey show educators how to create a climate where teachers are treated as the precious commodity that they are. New and veteran administrators and teachers alike can benefit from this quick read, and upon completion will be able to immediately implement culture-shifting strategies to improve their schools. Jeff and Tracey take you on a journey of self-reflection using stories educators can empathize with and learn from, while challenging you to take the next step in becoming ridiculously amazing!"

Beth Hench, Principal
Ayersville Elementary School
Defiance, Ohio

"*Ridiculously Amazing Schools* is a must-read for all educators wanting to create a culture that supports learning and social-emotional growth. It is not a typical 'do it my way' book. Instead, it asks you to take a courageous journey, and it gives you the tools and support to do just that. The practical and purposeful actions will resonate with all teachers who want to create a nurturing, supportive environment where everyone's needs are met. This would make a great book study in schools at each level, and I have no doubt it will be used over and over again by teachers and administrators as they begin their own courageous journey."

Ellen Cohan
Retired Associate Superintendent of Teaching and Learning
Forsyth County Schools, Georgia

"A unique and uplifting education book that focuses on how to support teachers in their quest to create ridiculously amazing schools. The key is investing in our people, their well-being, and the relationships we cultivate among them. The greatest impact on student learning are teachers and their belief in their impact. Jeff and Tracey provide conditions for success and practical guidance to help educators create schools students need. The time is now!"

Lissa Pijanowski, Ed.D.
Founder/Chief Learning Officer, Innovate 2 Educate and
Senior Fellow, International Center for Leadership in Education

RIDICULOUSLY
AMAZING SCHOOLS

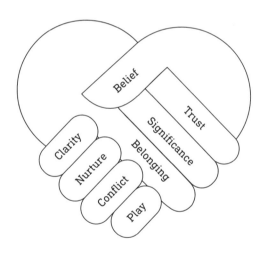

RIDICULOUSLY AMAZING SCHOOLS

CREATING A CULTURE
WHERE EVERYONE THRIVES

TRACEY SMITH AND JEFF WALLER

PUBLISH
YOUR
PURPOSE
PRESS

Books can be purchased at a bulk discount for educational use. For more information, contact 7 Mindsets at info@7mindsets.com.

Authors: Tracey Smith and Jeff Waller
Editor: Mandi Andrejka, PR with Panache!
Cover Design: Jeremy Turman, Global 360 Marketing
Project Management: Mahmoud Dahy
Educator Advisors: Sarah VonEsh, Ellen Cohan, MaryClaire Powell, and Derrick Hershey
Typeset by: Medlar Publishing Solutions Pvt Ltd., India

Lyrics in Chapter 7 used with permission of the team at Mashburn Elementary School, Forsyth County, GA.

Publisher: Publish Your Purpose Press
            141 Weston Street, #155
            Hartford, CT 06141

PUBLISH
YOUR
PURPOSE
PRESS

The opinions expressed by the Authors are not necessarily those held by Publish Your Purpose Press.

Printed in the United States of America.

ISBN: 978-1-946384-99-7 (hardcover)
ISBN: 978-1-951591-00-7 (paperback)
ISBN: 978-1-951591-01-4 (ebook)

Library of Congress Control Number: 2019916296

The information contained within this book is strictly for informational purposes. The material may include information, products, or services by third parties. As such, the Authors and Publisher do not assume responsibility or liability for any third-party material or opinions. The publisher is not responsible for websites (or their content) that are not owned by the publisher. Readers are advised to do their own due diligence when it comes to making decisions.

Publish Your Purpose Press works with authors, and aspiring authors, who have a story to tell and a brand to build. Do you have a book idea you would like us to consider publishing? Please visit PublishYourPurposePress.com for more information.

DEDICATION

To our courageous educators—the world-changers who brave our hallways and classrooms, who wholeheartedly give to our youth. By making one teacher or child better, even in the tiniest of ways, you make tomorrow a better and kinder place for all of us.

With great gratitude,

Tracey and Jeff

CONTENTS

HOW TO USE THIS BOOK

Ridiculously Amazing Schools provides a framework for improving the culture of your school. Our goal is to provide new insights and empower educators to take action that will drive real and meaningful impact. This book has been organized in a manner that facilitates putting these concepts into practical and purposeful action. It includes components that allow you to 1) assess the current state of your school's culture and 2) develop an informed plan to move forward successfully. It is our hope that this book acts as a reference guide that can be revisited to provide further direction as you progress.

ASSESSMENT TOOL

In each of the key sections of the book, you will find assessment questions. Additionally, you can find a complete Assessment Tool in the Appendix, along with a graphing tool to analyze the results. The Assessment Tool will provide you with an understanding of where you currently stand, as well as the biggest opportunities for improvements. An online version of the High-Level Assessment Tool is provided with a copy of this book. A school-wide Assessment Tool can also be obtained by emailing info@7Mindsets.com.

COMPANION GUIDE

The Appendix also includes a Companion Guide. This provides a framework for pulling ideas into one place in order to develop a plan. As you progress through each chapter, you will find a section called "Companion Guide Activity," where you can gather your thoughts and ideas from what you read.

PREFACE

This book comes from a journey we have collectively been on for over forty years. It's a journey that is not yet over, but through our struggles as educators and the hindering circumstances we've seen our fellow educators in, we felt compelled to share what we have come to understand along the way.

While we come at the lens of education from two very different angles, it's these combined views that have made our journey one of transformation. Jeff has worked with hundreds of schools over the past twenty years and assisted educators with implementing change and transforming culture. He has had the opportunity to see firsthand the challenge of education and the battlefield educators face every day. Jeff has been a student of the very best teachers and principals in the country.

Tracey has been an educator for twenty-two years, having spent the last eleven as a principal, eight of those at Mashburn Elementary, and most recently at Brookwood Elementary. She has experienced the great challenges of education, and has led and been a part of amazing educational teams. Through her experience, we have tried to ground the concepts of this book in reality and translate them into practical applications that will help you better succeed with your colleagues and students.

This book started with a single question. It is one we have been asking ourselves over the last decade of implementing social and emotional solutions in thirty-five states, interviewing hundreds of educators, observing thousands of classrooms, and partnering with an advisory team of more than thirty of the country's leading teachers and administrators. That question is this: What makes some schools and teachers courageous, and how are they thriving while so many schools and teachers are not?

That question has fascinated both of us for so long and started the journey that brought us together and inspired us to write this book. Together, we have observed amazing schools in all settings and age ranges. Likewise, we have witnessed extraordinary teachers in all of these environments. Teachers who are connected deeply with their students, teaching with rigor, and truly transforming lives.

Unfortunately, we have witnessed schools and colleagues struggling in these very same environments. Their days are not empowering and, more often than not, they go home feeling tired and frustrated. It became apparent to us that a large number of society's most important influencers—educators—are suffering. They are unhappy and feel disconnected and underappreciated.

In an attempt to understand the difference between those who are thriving and those who are not, we continued to ask the question. What we learned initially is what you already know. There are hundreds of situations happening each and every day that define the culture of a school. At first, it seemed there was no single answer. Success in a school was predicated on herculean efforts and the incredible vigilance of the administrators and teachers.

But as we dug deeper—below the depths of the day-to-day fires, at the very root of everything—we found the lever. We came to identify the one thing that, if done well, ripples out into everything that goes on in a school: if we as educators can rediscover each other and recognize and compel the greatness in one another, then we can change everything together.

INTRODUCTION

The most essential conclusion of our research is that you cannot teach the "whole" child without a "whole" teacher. For education to be at its best, we must create environments where our teachers can be at their best. Education is only as good as the teacher.

Tracey was recently at a restaurant, sitting outside with her family. It was chilly, and she was shivering and rubbing her arms to warm up. From behind, she felt someone put a jacket over her shoulders. She turned around to see a vaguely familiar face. The woman said, "I can see you're cold. Would you please take my jacket?" Not knowing exactly how to respond, Tracey gently declined and told the kind woman she was fine. She then got a rare and precious gift: it turned out the stranger was a parent of a former student from Mashburn Elementary School, where Tracey had been principal for eight years. She insisted Tracey take the jacket, saying, "You covered my family for so many years, please let me cover you."

It was a powerful moment for Tracey—one of those times when you get to see that all the struggle, the stress, and the heartbreak matter. It's a reminder that the promise of being an educator is still alive and well. Tracey immediately thought of her team.

She wished each of her teachers could feel the gratitude in this mother's heart. She desperately wanted them to feel the same pride that she had in that moment, knowing the difficult journey had been worth it. Her experiences at Mashburn and commitment to relationships first may not have always been easy, but they had led to a ridiculously amazing place for students, families, and teachers.

Educators are given a special gift: the ability for their work to transcend their own lives through the colleagues they work with and the students they teach. Unfortunately, the rewards can sometimes get lost in the tussle. We can lose sight of why we got into education in the first place. You see there is very little instant gratification. The fruits of great teaching may not be realized for decades. For many, the dream of teaching is greater than any moment of challenge. However, the work is not easy, and we have seen first-hand what it looks like.

When we surveyed educators as part of the research for this book, we often asked them what frustrated them. We observed a hidden, unfortunate conclusion: there are teachers and administrators who feel alone. Some principals feel like they have no one to talk to. There are no shoulders to cry on, no real emotional support structures in place within education. They feel like they are pitted against one another, and their work is so very public and transparent.

Some teachers feel disrespected by students and parents. They are fighting a battle that feels unwinnable. Every day is like a stage performance, and the show must always go on. Unlike other professions, they can't escape from the emotion by taking a long lunch or a day off when they have a bad day. And, to add even more pressure, one slip-up can have huge consequences.

We cannot allow this to continue. The members of one of our most essential professions must feel supported and must be put in a position to succeed.

So that brings us to the purpose of this book: addressing the needs of the adults in the building. This is not your grandmother's education book. This may be the first book you have ever read on education that does not focus on the student. This is not a book on leadership—there are already plenty of those out there. This isn't even a book on team building; however, it does go to the heart of great teams. This book is about relationships—not relationships with our students, but relationships among educators that define the culture within the school and the power we have to transform lives.

Karon Cunningham came to learn this at Franklin Middle School in Minneapolis, Minnesota. Morale was low and the school was mired in over 300 disciplinary referrals to the office. She instilled a culture of belief that recognized and celebrated the greatness in every team member and student in the building. Within one year, disciplinary referrals decreased by over 90%, and Franklin Middle School was outperforming other schools in the district. The students and teachers were even featured on *Good Morning America* and invited to the White House.

Beth Hench and Kirk Jones learned this at Ayersville Schools in Defiance, Ohio. They used some innovative programs to change the way they looked at each other and their students, and everything changed for the better. They implemented a new approach they called IMPACT. They enhanced their support for each other and started catching their students and teachers doing wonderful things and made it a source of celebration each and every day.

What Tracey, Karon, Kirk, and Beth have in common is they created a positive school culture where everyone can thrive. You can feel it when you walk into their buildings. Their staff meetings are magical. Their classrooms are lively. The hallways and even the bathrooms are inspirational. They have created ridiculously amazing schools, and we discovered how they did it.

It is said that you should listen to those coming back from where you want to go, as they may have insight on how to get there. That's what we hope to do here. We've spent decades working with some of the most powerful and inspirational educators in the country. We have observed, we have listened, we have been humbled; and they have enlightened us with the secret. It is our great hope that we have not only translated the beautiful minds of great educators around the country but that we have translated their extraordinary hearts as well.

That is the spirit of this book—to get us all to look around and recognize that by making our colleagues better, we make ourselves better, we give ourselves more meaning, and we better transform the lives of our students. We are confident that whether you come from a rural, urban, or suburban community, whether you serve elementary, middle, or high school students, this book can help you create a *ridiculously amazing school* where everyone can thrive.

COURAGEOUS SCHOOLS

The engineers who worked with Steve Jobs in the early days at Apple did not have favorable opinions of the work environment. The hours were long, the deadlines were unrealistic, and the demands were overwhelming. They remember being tired, stressed, and frustrated. But here's the catch: when asked if they missed it, every one of them wished they could go back. They longed to be in that room and part of a team completely committed to something they were passionate about and something that truly mattered.[1]

We see this in courageous schools. The work is hard and there is heartbreak and drama, but it means something. Educators know they are changing lives. They give it every ounce of everything they have. Some days are great, and others are a struggle. Many nights they go home tired and frustrated. Some may even dream of other careers. Thankfully, they wake up and get back to it the next day. And when the students show up, they have been able to muster

---

[1] Isaacson, *Steve Jobs*.

up the courage once again to be present, engaged, and energized for them.

There are many challenges in education, pressures and situations outside our control that make things difficult. According to Lee Shulman, "classroom teaching ... is perhaps the most complex, most challenging, and most demanding, subtle, nuanced, and frightening activity that our species has ever invented. In fact, when I compared the complexity of teaching with that much more highly rewarded profession, 'doing medicine,' I concluded that the only time medicine even approaches the complexity of an average day of classroom teaching is in an emergency room during a natural disaster."[2] We can all agree the work is hard, that educators see many things others are sheltered from, and that things happen that can weigh us down.

The truth is every school and every teacher has tragic stories that will break your heart. Students everywhere are experiencing real trauma, and they show up in our classrooms with a whole lot of baggage. We place many demands on our students, and many do not have their basic needs met. It is so hard to learn math when you are depressed, abused, or don't know what you're going to eat tonight or where you will sleep. The problems we see are so big, and there doesn't seem to be any real answers.

Yet we worked with courageous schools that are impacting these students. They are inspiring them to not repeat the cycle of their family members' lives and are quite possibly positioning them to solve the seemingly unsolvable problems we face. It isn't just the work of extraordinary individuals; courage seems to permeate every member of the team. Their collective mentality was

---

[2] Shulman, *Practice*, 504.

this: *When you are inside this building, we are going to feed you, we are going to love you, we are going to teach you, and we are going to change the trajectory of your life. We can't control what goes on out there, but we sure can control what happens when you walk through our doors.*

THE SOURCE OF COURAGE

So, where do these courageous educators and schools get their courage? How is it that they find the energy, the enthusiasm, the comfort, and the confidence to show up big time each and every day? Part of it is related to why they chose education in the first place. Most did it to impact lives and to help students overcome struggle and fulfill the great potential each and every one of them has. Many educators perform extraordinary acts on a daily basis simply because they truly care.

No mission, however, is big enough to sustain the level of excellence required to create a courageous school. No purpose is powerful enough to overcome repeated frustration or the futility of operating in a poorly functioning and unsupportive culture. There is something more, something that gets to the very heart of education. It's the fundamental element that dictates all the results we get in our classrooms and hallways.

As we observed these courageous schools, one variable stood out as the predictor of sustained excellence. It was not about geography, demographics, or pedagogy. It was not about leadership style or teaching practices. We have seen courageous schools in elementary, middle, and high schools. We have worked with courageous schools in inner cities, suburbia, and rural settings. It had nothing to do with any those elements; it had everything to do with relationships. While the relationships between educators and students are always important, what we have come to recognize as the foundation for a ridiculously amazing school is the manner in which the adults in the building relate to each other.

The problems our schools face can be solved through the hearts and minds of our educators, one teacher at a time. It's time to make our educators the heroes and allow them to rediscover their authentic greatness so they can connect with and empower every student to meet their fullest potential.

MOMENTS THAT MATTER

A recent analysis of a baseball game showed that in an average three-hour game, the total amount of time the ball is actually in play is about eight minutes. Those of you who have struggled making it through nine innings can appreciate this. Of those eight minutes, a much smaller fraction of that time is actually critical: when the ball is put in play or a pitch is made with the bases loaded. It's not that all the time warming up, strategizing, or practicing is not important, it's just that there are some moments that matter more. These are moments that will most define the outcomes we will get. It is in these moments that all our talents and efforts truly express themselves. It is in these moments that we can redefine ourselves and change the culture of the game.

When we look at courageous relationships in schools—colleagues who truly support and empower one another—we try to understand how they got there. We ask these educators to define the source of the bond that makes everyone better. They talk with us about topics such as trust, compassion, respect, and competence. But where do those elements come from? What is at the very heart of a courageous relationship?

When we dig deeper, it almost invariably goes to specific events. Moments in time when a word or action changed everything and set the relationship on the pathway to courage. One teacher shared with us how much she respected her principal. It started early in the principal's career when a good friend of the principal had been hired but was a toxic influence throughout the school. The principal found her courage, transitioned the friend, and then met with the staff to reinforce that she would not accept disrespectful treatment from anyone. That was a defining moment for every educator in the school. It showed that the principal, no matter how difficult the situation, was willing to step up when it came to the greater good of the rest of the team.

A coach shared with us a time he had come to work after hearing his father had been diagnosed with cancer. The football team was practicing for the region championship the next day, and he did not want to let the head coach down. When the head coach passed him in the hallway, he could see by this man's body language that something was wrong. The head coached inquired and learned of the father's sickness. He told the assistant, "You will be a coach here for many years, but you only have one father." Not only that, the head coach said he would work with the administration to get his classes covered and ensure his role on the team was filled until he had taken care of his dad.

There are 180 days in a school year. The average educator spends over 1,500 hours inside the four walls of their school. The vast majority of that time is spent planning or with students. If you boil it down, educators spend less than fifty hours a year in direct interaction with their colleagues. And, like baseball, a fraction of this time is critical. These are the moments when what we do matters more. We must learn to recognize them. We must find the resolve to be at our best, fully present, and engaged with empathy and courage. If we don't recognize and take advantage of these moments, we allow things to stay the same. If we do lean in, these moments transform lives and the culture of our schools.

Courage is not only performing great acts of valor—in fact, that is not at all what it is in education. Courage is the ability to be engaged and to act with consistency and power during all these critical moments. Everything we do matters, and the words we use and the feelings we have toward each other are critical. What is that word or action going to be, and what type of impact are we going to have? We owe it to ourselves and to each other to put our colleagues in a position to be their most powerful and authentic selves.

The struggle is real for all of us, but if we want to win with the students, we have to first win with the teachers. The only way we can truly transform schools is with, for, and through one another. The first and most important task of an educational team is creating an environment where every teacher can be courageous in these critical moments. It's through our relationships with our team that we find the courage we need, and collectively we can then become a courageous school.

FOSTERING EDUCATOR SOCIAL AND EMOTIONAL HEALTH

Transforming education will be predicated on our ability to enable our educators to find their authentic power, to be excited, engaged, confident, and comfortable. Success in that one area can transform every other aspect of education.

If you look at the typical course load in education colleges around the country, you will find a curriculum focused mainly on instructional strategies, lesson planning, student teaching, and educational theory. Some may branch out a bit and discuss relationship development with students, but rarely do they talk about building relationships with colleagues and creating effective teams. Teachers too often do not see themselves as important members of the school learning community.

For the educators who go to grad school and aspire to become building-level leaders, they learn about working with state budgets, educational law, and hiring practices. Some even teach educators how to fire someone, but very few—if any—talk about how to nurture and develop teachers or how to build empowered teams that collectively transform school culture and student lives.

A lack of effective support and investment in these relationships inhibits our ability to keep our best educators and engage our students with rigor. Most people don't even realize that one of the biggest challenges holding a school back is the lack of social and emotional health of the adults in the building. When the relationships we have with one another are strained, the quality of the education we provide to our students suffers.

In the *Tao Te Ching*, Lao Tzu said that governing a large country is like frying a fish. If you poke it too much, you will spoil it. The same can be said for running a large organization: if you touch it too much, you will ruin it. We have overengineered education. Too many really smart people have come up with clever concepts and models. We have created policies and implemented practices, and our schools have become overly analytical and data-driven organizations. We have lost focus on the relationships and the importance they have in driving the outcomes we are measuring.

We keep looking for answers in policies, procedures, and new pedagogy, yet that is not where the answers live. There will always be new ways to teach and new technology, but how helpful can they really be if we keep throwing one new thing after another at an already overburdened team? The solution we've seen work is to strengthen our educators' abilities to connect with others so they can function at higher levels individually and collectively, as well as work through challenges feeling supported.

This is the critical shift that we believe is essential for schools to become courageous: a focus on the inner workings of the adults in the building. Relationships among the team are the base of every successful organization and school. If we want our teachers to empower and inspire, we must help them become empowered and inspired. If we create the pathway to build courageous relationships, we will create a culture that attracts, develops, and keeps the very best educators among us—a culture that empowers every student to fulfill their authentic potential.

THE THREE CONDITIONS OF COURAGE

What does it take to truly be a passionate educator?

Think about a situation where you feel you are at your best: You are present and fully engaged in the moment. You are confident, comfortable, energized, and excited by what you are doing. Perhaps you are simply hanging out with friends or loved ones, or perhaps you are in your element at school. It is in these moments that we are at our greatest creative capacity and we are performing and functioning at our highest level. We experience great joy and meaning and we have positive impact.

Mihaly Csikszentmihalyi, author of *Flow: The Psychology of Optimal Experience*, describes this state of being as "flow." His primary conclusion is that our happiness and overall achievement in life is directly correlated to our ability to attain a state of flow as much as we possibly can.[3] It is this state that we want our teachers in as they walk our hallways and empower our children.

---

[3] Csikszentmihalyi, *Creativity*, 2–4.

The question is how to get them there. What can we do as a team to maximize the potential and impact of every educator in the building? How do we give them the **courage** to be their very best at those critical moments, when so much can be at stake, and the future of our students' lives is being forged?

THE COURAGEOUS RELATIONSHIP

Courage is found in our commitment to the students. However, courage is magnified and sustained through the relationships we have with our colleagues. These are the courageous relationships that will drive the thriving school culture we seek.

Courage exists in all of us. We are all born with it, and it presents itself within each of us to varying degrees. Education itself can be a source of great courage. We can find strength in knowing we have the rare and precious opportunity to transform lives and build something truly extraordinary. There is more, however, that we need to do to intentionally build courage.

To have sustainable courage, the kind that drives everyone to new levels, requires community. It is the courage you feel on that day when things at home are a mess and you don't know if you can muster up the energy to truly be there for your students. You find that courage in that moment when a colleague recognizes your struggle and takes time to listen to you, to empathize with you, and perhaps even takes your class for a few moments while you regroup. It is the courage you gain when someone disagrees with you, but rather than letting it fester, they approach you with grace to talk it out. The conversation is not comfortable, but it is creative, energizing, and empowering. It is the courage you gain when a colleague recognizes something good about you and expresses their appreciation to you.

Courage in a school is conditional. Schools can intentionally foster an environment where every teacher can find their power, where we can be our best in the critical moments that will ultimately define us. There are three conditions that must exist within our relationships that create courage and allow us to thrive—trust, significance, and belonging. These three conditions are fundamental professional needs for all of us. These same conditions will dictate the quality of a culture that exists within a given school. Our ability to create empowered teams is based on our ability to build relationships that foster trust, while creating a sense of significance and belonging among each team member.

COURAGEOUS CONDITION #1:
TRUST

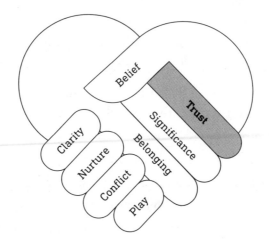

Think about a time in your life when you were in a relationship that lacked trust. How did it make you feel? Were you likely to take initiative or be open and constructive? Did you spend time thinking about what the other person was telling others about you or what they were saying behind your back? Did you enjoy the relationship or did you tolerate it? Did that person give you energy or drain you like a vampire?

Now think about a time in your life when you had a truly trusting relationship with someone else. Possibly a parent, a sibling, or a great friend or colleague. You might have gone to them with your struggles and celebrations. They understood you, knew you at a personal level, and cared about you. What was that like? How was it different than a relationship without trust?

As we interviewed Ellen Cohan, longtime teacher, administrator, and educational consultant, she concluded, "Everything is about trust; that is where it starts and ends in education." In fact, when we dug in with every educator we interviewed, one concept that continued to come up was trust. Almost everyone agreed it to be elusive yet critical to building a thriving culture. It was at the very heart of creating constructive relationships, forging powerful educational teams, and promoting growth individually and collectively.

Trust is so critical. It is the foundation around which human relationships are centered. It allows us to feel safe, to feel like we are part of something. It's the glue that keeps us together and allows us to collectively move forward. Trust allows communities to flourish, while lack of trust causes division, conflict, and struggle.

When we ask an educator to be courageous, we are asking them to take risks, to be vulnerable, and to put themselves in a situation that is possibly uncomfortable in the beginning. Educators cannot do any of these things without confidence in the people and circumstances around them. They need to know that it's okay to make mistakes, that a platform of support exists, and that others have the best of intentions for them and their work.

When there is trust, educators are excited and eager to volunteer and contribute their talents, energy, and honest constructive thinking. If the level of trust is low, they may limit their involvement. They're much less likely to contribute ideas and volunteer. Time may get wasted on building politics, and the full force of educators' passions and skills will not be realized or recognized.

GRADING YOURSELF

Is trust a source of courage in your school? Take this brief assessment individually or as a team to determine if your team trusts one another. The first three questions are designed to gauge the level of trust you feel, while the last question will be your summary score that you can plot in the complete Assessment Tool provided in the Appendix.

Quiz Question (Circle the grade that applies)	
I trust the members of my team.	A B C D F
I feel members of the team trust me.	A B C D F
I feel like I am authentic and genuine at work.	A B C D F
My overall Trust Score is:	**A B C D F**

Note: The online version of the full high-level assessment is provided free with this book at www.7mindsets.com/RAS. A school-wide Assessment Tool can be used school-wide by emailing info@7mindsets.com.

COURAGEOUS CONDITION #2:
SIGNIFICANCE

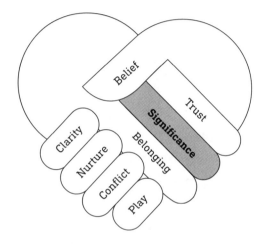

Teacher attrition is becoming an epidemic in education. In fact, when we interviewed superintendents, two factors that they say keep them up at night are student achievement and teacher turnover. According to the National Center of Education Statistics' survey in 2013, about 8% of teachers had transferred to a new school the prior year and another 8% left the profession altogether.[4] Worse yet, in high-poverty schools where there are already minimal resources, teachers are nearly twice as likely to exit.[5] In another study done by the *American Educational Research*

[4] Goldring et al., "Teacher Attrition."

[5] National Center for Education Statistics, "Teacher Turnover."

Journal, it was concluded that in some states, a full 62% of teachers have left the school where they began within the first three years.[6]

A survey by the Organisation for Economic Co-operation and Development reported that while nine out of ten teachers feel satisfied with their profession, more than two-thirds of teachers do not feel their profession is valued by society. And this isn't limited to teachers in the United States. More than 100,000 teachers and school leaders from thirty-four countries participated in the survey.[7]

Additionally, a study from Penn State claims that among professional occupations, teachers rate lowest in feeling that their opinions count at work.[8] Far too many teachers go home on a regular basis not feeling good about the work they do or what they contribute. Fewer and fewer educators feel like they matter or that they are respected and appreciated by those they work with and for. The impact of this inconsistency and uncertainty can be extremely damaging to the culture of a school and the students they teach.

Thousands of young teachers enter the field every year, only to find the experience very different than what they expected. The work is hard, the environment isn't always supportive, and they may be asked to do tasks that aren't that enjoyable—or don't technically fall under their job descriptions. But worst of all, they are not thriving, they do not feel good about what they do, and they do not feel appreciated by their colleagues. Throw on top of this a moderate salary, and you can understand why some teachers leave the industry shortly after entering it.

---

[6] Redding and Henry, "School."

[7] Organisation for Economic Co-operation and Development, "Teachers."

[8] Greenberg et al., "Teacher Stress."

Many years ago, in our work developing student social and emotional solutions, we came across the work of Jane Nelson. Nelson authored many books on positive discipline based on the theories of Alfred Adler and Rudolf Dreikurs. One of the key principles of her work was the need for every child to feel a sense of belonging and significance.[9] For a child to truly thrive, they must feel they matter, and they must feel like they are part of a community. If they do not, they will suffer and open themselves up to a whole host of pitfalls.

Our research and experience have concluded that the same can be said for all of us. To inspire, we must become inspired. To make others feel safe, we must feel safe. To help others feel a sense of significance, we must first feel that for ourselves. As the book written by Neila A. Connors so aptly says, "If we don't feed the teachers, they eat the students."[10] If we do feed the teachers, however, we will help them fulfill their potential as educators and transform the lives of their students in the process.

In our opinion, no profession in the world has more purpose than education. Educators are building the future and have the opportunity every day to transform lives. But that sense of purpose is not enough to keep every teacher engaged and thriving. Too many teachers go home most days feeling poorly about their contribution. If you do not feel good about your work on a daily basis, if you do not feel significant, you will become frustrated and demoralized.

Feeling insignificant can be devastating. When people don't feel significant, they are less likely to engage—at work, at home, or

---

[9] Nelson et al., *Positive Discipline*.

[10] Connors, *Teachers*.

in their community. Consider a time in your life when you knew your talents and efforts were appreciated. Now consider a time when you did not feel respected or acknowledged. The differences we see in ourselves when we feel significant can be everything.

Thriving schools are effective at making team members feel significant. In a thriving school, educators are appreciated for their uniqueness and provided opportunities to share and express themselves in powerful ways. Efforts are made to put each team member into roles and projects where their unique talents and interests will shine. Opinions and ideas are welcomed and incorporated in the day-to-day operations. Individuals and teams are supported, celebrated, and recognized. There are constantly new opportunities to develop capacities and competencies.

GRADING YOURSELF

Is significance a source of courage in your school? Take this brief assessment individually or as a team to determine if you feel empowered. The first three questions are designed to gauge the level of significance you feel, while the last question will be your summary score that you can plot in the complete Assessment Tool provided in the Appendix.

Quiz Question (Circle the grade that applies)					
I feel like I am very good at the work I do.	A	B	C	D	F
I am recognized appropriately for my contributions.	A	B	C	D	F
Most nights, I go home feeling good about the impact I have at my job.	A	B	C	D	F
My overall Significance Score is:	**A**	**B**	**C**	**D**	**F**

Note: The online version of the full high-level assessment is provided free with this book at www.7mindsets.com/RAS. A school-wide Assessment Tool can be used school-wide by emailing info@7mindsets.com.

COURAGEOUS CONDITION #3: BELONGING

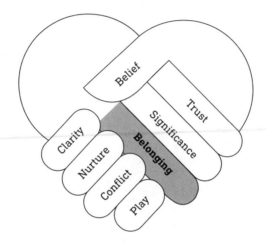

Cheers was a popular TV show in the 1980s and 1990s. It was the story of some working-class regulars of a Boston bar called Cheers who simply shared life experiences and lives with each other. To this day, many people find themselves singing the lyrics from the catchy theme song: "Sometimes you want to go where everybody knows your name and they're always glad you came." Feeling a sense of belonging is essential to human happiness and is critical to our functioning and performance.

In a *Psychology Today* article, Dr. Karyn Hall defined belonging as "acceptance as a member or part."[11] A sense of belonging is a human need just like the need for food and shelter. Feeling that

---

[11] Hall, "Belonging."

you belong is necessary in order to see value in life and cope with intensely painful emotions.

The opposite of belonging is loneliness. Gregory Walton, a social psychologist and assistant professor at Stanford University, has executed a series of studies on the impact of loneliness and the importance of belonging. According to Walton, feeling like we belong to a greater community that shares common interests and goals strongly impacts our interests, motivations, health, and happiness. In fact, research shows that IQ test performance, sense of well-being, and self-control can all be undermined from even one situation of feeling excluded.[12]

Consider a time in your life when you felt like an outsider. For many, we simply go back to our time in middle or high school. What was it like? Did you feel like you could be yourself? Was it easy to relate to others and find common ground? Did you enjoy being with them? Could you possibly be at your best?

Now consider a time when you found your stride within a group or organization. You could make mistakes, stumble and fall, and the environment was not only forgiving, it was affirming. You could laugh comfortably at yourself. You felt like you were in your element, that your flaws were endearing, and you could even lose track of time in the presence of positive interaction. You could take risks, you could be authentic, and you genuinely looked forward to hanging out with others.

Education is a highly relational profession. Like any great team, we are improved when we understand one another. It allows us to find connection points and to see and appreciate that we are all on the same journey together. When we connect with others at

---

[12] Enayati, "Belonging."

a personal level, we perform and function at a higher level. It makes us happier, and happy teachers truly do create happy students.

Creating a strong sense of belonging among all team members is foundational to a thriving culture. People will fight through adversity and make personal sacrifices for the collective good when operating in a strong supportive community. Courageous schools foster connection and community among their educators. It's important for teachers to have opportunities to get to know and appreciate one another on a personal level, to feel like they have each other's backs, and to constructively challenge one another to be the best versions of themselves.

People often leave their jobs because they don't feel appreciated; however, they'll put up with much and put forth extraordinary effort when they feel like a part of a caring community. Creating a sense of belonging is the platform for higher levels of collaboration and creativity, as well as for individual and collective growth. It relaxes us to be ourselves, it brings us into the moment, it heightens our senses, and it empowers us to thrive. It is a fundamental condition of courage.

GRADING YOURSELF

Is belonging a source of courage in your school? Take this brief assessment individually or as a team to determine if you have a strong sense of community within your school. The first three questions are designed to gauge the level of belonging you feel, while the last question will be your summary score that you can plot in the complete Assessment Tool provided in the Appendix.

Quiz Question (Circle the grade that applies)					
When I am with my colleagues, I feel like I belong.	A	B	C	D	F
I feel there is a great sense of community among the staff.	A	B	C	D	F
I look forward to the interactions with my team.	A	B	C	D	F
My overall Belonging Score is:	**A**	**B**	**C**	**D**	**F**

Note: The online version of the full high-level assessment is provided free with this book at www.7mindsets.com/RAS. A school-wide Assessment Tool can be used school-wide by emailing info@7mindsets.com.

BUILDING THE COURAGEOUS RELATIONSHIP

Like air and water are to life, trust, significance,
and belonging are to thrive. We simply cannot
be our best authentic selves if these conditions
do not exist for us within the school.

To truly be a courageous educator, to continually face and push through struggles, to maintain the vigilance to press on and sustain, we must feel powerful. We are powerful when we are grounded in our authentic self—when our energy levels are high, our attention is heightened, and confidence flows through us. These conditions cannot manifest where a sense of trust, belonging, and significance do not exist.

Based on our experience, interviews, and research, we identified five elements courageous schools have that can cultivate these three conditions. These five elements will provide a deeper understanding and deliver proven approaches to increase the courage of your school. As you read these, you may recognize that your school already has many of the qualities and you may realize others are lacking. No school is perfect, and even the best have room for improvement. The ability to recognize and improve these five elements within your school will ensure you continue to have a greater impact on the educators and students in your building.

BELIEF

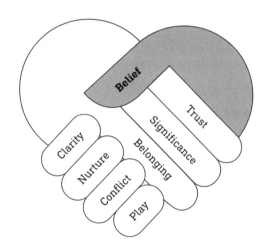

BELIEF
SEEING THE HIGHER PART OF THINGS

If we look at things differently, the things that we look at will be different. If we can see what is good and wonderful in each other and the situations we are in, then those are the things that will grow and expand.

Recently, we heard a story of a famous train ride in New York. A father was on a train with his young son. The boy was likely four or five years old. He was curious and kept pointing at things, exclaiming over and over again, "What is that?" His father would smile and gently say, "That's a tree," or "That is a train, like the one we're in."

At first, the curiosity was cute to the other passengers, but the boy kept asking questions. Not only that, the boy's voice was getting louder and louder. It was a long train ride, and after an extended period of incessant question-asking, one woman in particular began getting frustrated.

It started to feel rude. Why was the father not being considerate of the other passengers? The boy was cute, but it had been a long day and everyone on the train wanted to relax a little. She approached the father, tired and frustrated. She asked the father to please calm the boy down, saying that his energy level was too high and it was very distracting to the other passengers who were trying to wind down after a long day.

The father looked up, shocked. He had been so focused on his son; he had not been aware of the impact they were having on the other passengers. "I am so sorry," he said. "We just got out of corrective eye surgery, and this is the first time my son has ever been able to really see." The father had been so caught up in the joy and excitement of the miracle that he got lost in the moment.

As you could imagine, the woman felt awful. She simply had no idea of the situation, but she let her frustration get the best of her. We look at the world through a lens that is largely based on past conditioning. We make assumptions and we make judgments. These judgments and assumptions always lack perspective and complete information. But we act on them and we often do damage to ourselves and others.

Belief is the perspective of seeing the higher part of each other and the situation we are in. It means that when a colleague shows up late, we don't immediately assume the worst. It means we believe in them and ask ourselves to look at this situation with a different lens. Maybe someone the colleague cares about is sick or injured, or possibly they have an urgent personal matter they must deal with.

When we approach them, we approach them from this new perspective. Rather than accusing them or interrogating them, we come at the conversation with empathy. You might ask, "Is everything okay?" It is not that you don't address the issue, you just do it from a foundation of belief. You might add, "I noticed you have been coming in late, and I wanted to make sure everything was okay."

Had the woman on the train come at the conversation from a different perspective, everything would have been different. She saw it from her own perspective but lacked all the information. Perhaps she could have started the conversation off with, "Your son sure has a lot of curiosity." The father would have likely shared that the child had just had corrective eye surgery. The woman's

heart would have warmed and the situation would have gone much differently—it would have been much better.

Courageous schools foster a culture of belief. When you observe them, there is a capacity among the team to see the better parts of each other and to look at situations from a lens of optimism and high expectations. It is so important that we see the higher part of each other so we can all see that within ourselves. It builds relationships and it makes us feel confident, competent, and supported. It's true that we will rise or fall to the expectations we have for ourselves and for each other.

THE COURAGE OF BELIEF

Why It Is Hard

Why is it so hard for us to see the best in others? That was the question we asked Howard Glasser, the creator of the Nurtured Heart Approach. In the early 1990s, his therapy practice worked with some of the most difficult and challenging children in Tucson, Arizona. He began getting results no one else was getting, and seeing breakthroughs with children who had experienced some of the very worst forms of trauma. His process is simple: if we can train ourselves to see and recognize the greatness in someone, we will empower them to see and believe in that greatness, and that can propel them into a process of growth and fulfillment of their potential. Over the years, Howard has learned that the process that is so potent with children is equally as powerful and transformative with adults.

When asked why it's so hard for most of us to see someone's greatness, he told us how seductive the inner critic is in all of us. There is a gravitational force that has evolved in us for hundreds of generations that pulls us toward those parts of others that frustrate us, that we disagree with, and that we feel are somehow lacking or flawed. Worse yet, this force seeks others who are likeminded to join into the gossip and criticism. It is an unfortunate aspect of human nature.

Howard himself has been practicing his approach for thirty years, yet he fights the seduction of the inner critic each and every day. This critic mindset permeates our culture, and you really have to swim upstream to be one of those people who sees the higher part of others. He has mantras he tells himself time and time again to keep himself away from the current of negative discourse. This is difficult, even for someone like Howard who has committed his profession to it and practiced his entire life at perfecting belief.

Moreover, many people we interviewed talked about education having a very comparative and competitive culture among its professionals. Sometimes educators are their own worst enemies, comparing their school or classroom to their colleagues—possibly finding resentment, anger, and even insecurity when putting themselves side by side with others. This further magnifies our differences, creates dissention, and erodes our trust in each other.

In our schools, it is very difficult to have the presence and mindfulness to see the best in others. What we disagree with, don't like, or differ with is electric. It pops out subconsciously with no effort at all. The seductive force of the critic takes over, and we channel our thoughts toward the negative. We find ourselves continually rediscovering the critic within. Without intentionality, this drives what we think about, and that is what we talk about with our like-minded colleagues.

BELIEF MATTERS

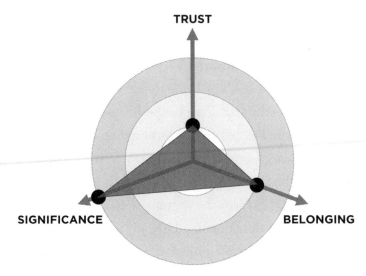

Courage Contribution

- Fostering **Belief** will primarily drive **Significance**. As colleagues recognize and affirm one another, all will feel more competent and capable.

- Secondarily, it will promote a sense of **Belonging**. Being recognized and acknowledged makes us feel a part of the team and connects us with our colleagues.

- Finally, **Trust** will be improved. Seeing and expecting more from others increases our confidence in ourselves and others.

We must rediscover one another, find the greatness in each other, and empower each other to see and fulfill the great potential within ourselves.

Many times, funerals include the celebration of a person's life. People get up and share amazing stories and celebrate the character and qualities of the deceased. You talk with friends and loved ones, and you laugh and cry about the times you were touched by the individual. You might wonder if anyone ever said this while the person was alive. What a shame it would be if they left this Earth not knowing. How many people have moved on without truly knowing how much people cared?

We almost always wait until it is too late to see the best in another human being. We care about them, and they probably know it, but we rarely put it into words or truly caring action before the opportunity has passed. Imagine how powerful and invigorating it would be if everyone saw the best in us and took the time to recognize the best part of us. If we could see the better part in each other, we would make ourselves and everyone around us better.

We work with many psychologists who help individuals but also work with couples. There is a common practice in relationship or couples' therapy. Psychologists will ask people in struggling relationships to identify the things they like or the higher parts of one another. This simple practice can be transformative.

It is said that energy flows where attention goes. Things we focus on expand in our lives. If we focus on the negatives, they expand and become more problematic. If we take our attention to the positives, they become the foundation of positive and powerful growth. By intentionally taking our attention to the parts of each other we like or admire, we transform the energy in the relationship. We make the positives the foundation of growth. We begin to appreciate each other more and feel appreciated to a greater extent.

Imagine a colleague coming up to you and mentioning an interaction she saw between you and a student. In a critical moment, she shares how impressed she is at your ability to connect and get the most out of your students. In fact, she would like to sit down with you and pick your brain about how she can be better. Imagine a new teacher who speaks up in a staff meeting for the first time. The principal pauses and says, "Thank you for sharing. You have a powerful voice, and I really hope you continue to speak up and share your ideas in the future." What would the impact be on us as educators if we put our biggest energy on what was working rather than on what we perceived to be broken?

Now consider you are having a bad day. You say something you regret, and a few days later, you go meet with administration. In this essential moment, rather than attacking you, they start off by saying, "We've seen you in class and we know how compassionate you are. What's going on? Is there anything we can do to help?" How different would your response be if that were the case? How much more committed would you be to your team? How much better would you be for your colleagues and students in the future?

Collective Teacher Efficacy (CTE) is the school staff's collective belief in their ability to positively affect students. John Hattie and his team have presented CTE as the "new number one influence" related to student achievement.[13] When we foster a culture of belief, not only will culture and morale improve, but so will student achievement.

We all want to be in a place where we are celebrated, not simply tolerated. We need to make school a place where we applaud the differences and the best parts of one another. Ultimately, the culture we create is driven by the expectations we have, the words we use, and the actions we take. Our schools need to intentionally build a culture of belief. We need to rediscover the greatness

---

[13] Visible Learning, "Collective Teacher Efficacy (CTE)."

within and reconnect more deeply with the passion that drove us to become educators.

In many ways, belief is the trickiest of the elements for courageous relationships. Yet it might just be the most powerful. In our opinion, it goes against generations of conditioning. Our ability to see the higher part of our colleagues and expect greatness is so important. It not only empowers us, but strengthens relationships and is a primary driver of trust. It also fosters a strong sense of belonging and empowers all team members to feel a sense of contribution and significance.

BELIEF IN ACTION

Derrick Hershey is a high school math teacher turned elementary school principal. The leadership in his district—Forsyth County, Georgia—has inspired him to always put relationships first. Essential to that is creating a team that supports one another.

He shared with us a turning point in his educational career. While at church, a speaker talked about the concept of "catching" someone. If you poll the average person, especially a teacher, "catching" means to see someone in the act of doing something wrong. This speaker used a clever play on words about how we need to think of each other and create supportive communities. We need to catch each other in support and belief, not catch each other doing things wrong.

Derrick told us that, many days, his teachers come in burdened. Things are going on in their lives outside of the school that have significant impact on their emotions. He decided the team would create a culture of catching one another by embracing them during a fall, providing support, and making sure they find a space to be effective with their students each day. It became part of their ethos.

The genius in this concept is altering the default lens of the educators in the building. For example, if there is a teacher who is repeatedly coming in late, our default lens goes to seeing the worst part of them, frustrated that they are incapable of showing up on time and angry that we have to cover for them. With a catching culture, we flip the switch and teach ourselves to assume the best. The first step is to cover his or her class with grace. Maybe she is on the phone with a parent, or perhaps he has a serious personal issue of his own. We need to give others the benefit of the doubt, and come at it from a perspective of compassion.

It is so critical that our educator teams understand that we are all human and that we all have good and bad days. In every courageous school we observed, there was a cultural norm that ensured a supportive mindset among the staff. In the complex drama-filled world of education, it is so easy for divisiveness to spread. We must create models that combat dissention and isolation and promote a supportive team. We must recognize and reward this behavior and make school a safe place where teachers can be at their best.

GRADING YOURSELF

Is belief a strength in your school? Take this brief assessment individually or as a team to determine if you believe in one another. The first five questions are designed to gauge the level of belief you feel, while the last question will be your summary score that you can plot in the complete Assessment Tool provided in the Appendix.

Quiz Question (Circle the grade that applies)					
My colleagues are talented and care deeply about their jobs.	A	B	C	D	F
My school is in the process of doing great things for its staff and students.	A	B	C	D	F
My colleagues and I celebrate our differences.	A	B	C	D	F
We work to include different perspectives in the key decisions we make.	A	B	C	D	F
I feel empowered by my colleagues.	A	B	C	D	F
My overall Belief Score is:	**A**	**B**	**C**	**D**	**F**

Note: The online version of the full high-level assessment is provided free with this book at www.7mindsets.com/RAS. A school-wide Assessment Tool can be used school-wide by emailing info@7mindsets.com.

THE TIME IS NOW
Proven Practices to Start Building Belief Today

Celebrate Successes

The things we focus on expand. When we see the lower part of each other and bring attention to those qualities, we tend to see those very qualities expand in each other. The best way to bring out the best in ourselves and each other is to see and celebrate the best within us.

Schools we work with around the country have added an agenda item at the end of their staff meetings: they celebrate one another. Sometimes team members celebrate publicly. Sometimes they are asked to write something down and share a note, and sometimes they break into small teams and express gratitude to one another.

We live in a world where it is so easy to judge and criticize. We must be intentional about creating spaces where we can learn to see the best part of others. It really is a matter of perspective, and we choose what we focus on.

When you find the greatness in your colleagues, they feel supported and valued. This begins to build partnerships among you. When teachers feel safe to take risks in the classroom, they can then feel the freedom to allow their students to also take those same risks.

Perform Showers of Praise

Why wait until someone retires or passes away to celebrate them? There is a technique we have seen used called the Shower of Praise. A staff member is randomly selected to stand in front of the team, and their colleagues take turns celebrating what is great about them. You can spice it up by role-playing that the person is retiring today. Imagine they are leaving the school for good. What would you want to thank them for before they left?

This can be so powerful in getting team members to see the better part of their colleagues. You can do this in a large group or within smaller teams. The goal would be to get every staff member celebrated at least once a year. This process connects the team and fosters a sense of belonging. It is also a very affirming process to help people feel appreciated and celebrated among the team.

Thank It Forward

Leading researcher Dr. Martin E. P. Seligman, a psychologist at the University of Pennsylvania, tested the impact of various positive psychology interventions on 411 people. When their week's assignment was to write and personally deliver a letter of gratitude to someone who had never been properly thanked for his or her kindness, participants immediately exhibited a huge increase in happiness scores. This impact was greater than that from any other intervention, with benefits lasting for a month.[14]

It is said that gratitude is the gift that gives twice, once to the giver and once to the receiver. There is something so powerful about expressing gratitude. It connects people, it makes us feel appreciated, and it fosters greater levels of overall grace in all of us.

---

[14] Seligman and Steen, "Psychology."

Find ways to create spaces in the busy school schedule to thank each other. One idea is to ask teachers to send thank you notes or texts each day to colleagues who helped them out. You could find time at the end of meetings to have educators pair up and express what they appreciate about each other. The key is to find a mechanism to have colleagues search for and express the higher part of each other whenever possible.

Celebrate Perfect Imperfections

Social media and other outlets can be incredibly harmful to what we believe is the reality for others. We can never compete with people's highlight reels on these sites—nor should we. When you embrace "Perfectly Imperfect" you begin to realize that you, and everyone around you, are not perfect, nor should you be. When teachers at Mashburn Elementary embraced this concept a few years ago, it changed the relationships they had with each other as well as with their students and their families. Life's challenges happen to everyone. No one escapes them. When we go into a conversation knowing that each person is trying to overcome some personal challenge, it creates a common ground. This also gives you some grace when you make a mistake—own it and see how you can use this opportunity to strengthen the relationship instead of letting it tear you apart.

Likewise, on a great team where there is a lot of trust and mutual respect, you can share your ideas without the fear of judgment. Some of your best ideas can come from your worst ideas. Create a safe space for bad ideas and let these ideas evolve and grow. If you're afraid of being shot down, then chances are you won't ever take the leap necessary to throw out a truly radical idea. Be good at being wrong and create an environment where

42

those around you can take chances without the fear of judgment or failure.

Change the Narrative

Aaron Beck is regarded as the father of cognitive therapy and is famous for pioneering theories widely used in the treatment of depression. He developed the concept of negative automatic thoughts, which fuel many of us. There are several different names for this concept, and some schools call them Automatic Negative Thoughts or ANTs.

There are fun and engaging activities schools can do to reduce the negative dialogue among teachers and students. One clever strategy is a "Stomp out the ANTS" campaign. Whenever you catch yourself or a colleague talking or thinking negatively, stomp your foot on the ground. Now that the ANT is dead, you can change words, thinking, and action to one of belief and higher expectations.

Other schools we work with have "Flip the Switch" programs. George Couros, a high school principal turned speaker, has a saying: you need to make the positives so loud that the negatives are almost impossible to hear. Don't let the few negative people rain on your parade. When you are tempted to be the one who goes to the negative, stop yourself and flip it. If you are the one who is experiencing the effects of someone who is negative, first look for what you can do to manage your own emotions, and then look to those who are positive and seek their attention and feedback.

Make the motion or imagine flipping the switch—turning the negative off and turning the positive on. If we can change the narrative in the hallways, classrooms, and recesses of our own minds, we can foster belief in ourselves and our colleagues.

Build a Greatness Chain

Methany Thornton at Marietta Middle School used a tool—a simple notebook—to celebrate the greatness of her colleagues. To start off, she would identify a colleague and write a journal entry that expressed appreciation for the contributions this team member was making to the school. She then posed a challenge to her colleague to do the same for someone working in the math department at the school. The colleague would follow suit, expressing appreciation of another colleague's greatness and then posing a challenge for them to do the same. After a few months, the notebook was full. Instead of ending the greatness chain there, Methany put that notebook on a shelf, calling it Volume 1, so that it could be referenced and enjoyed in the future. She then started a new notebook to continue the greatness chain indefinitely.

This is a powerful way of reinforcing the greatness in each other and expanding belief. If you want to take it to the next level, instead of simply expressing appreciation, ask the team to do three things when adding their link to the chain:

1. State what is great or wonderful about your colleague.
2. State what he or she means to you.
3. State what that says about your colleague as a person and educator.

COMPANION GUIDE ACTIVITY:
FOSTERING BELIEF

Belief is the perspective of seeing the higher part of each other. In many ways, belief is the trickiest of the catalysts for courageous relationships, yet it might just be the most powerful. It goes against human nature and generations of conditioning. Our ability to see the higher part of our colleagues and expect greatness is a primary driver of trust in ourselves and those we work with. It also fosters a strong sense of belonging and empowers all team members to feel a sense of contribution and significance.

Organization: What organizational changes or adjustments should be made (new roles or team structures)?

_____

_____

_____

_____

People: What professional development, book studies, and self-paced learning should be added?

_____

_____

_____

_____

Process: What activities can be added or integrated within the current schedule?

_____

_____

_____

_____

Technology and Tools: How can we leverage technology and tools?

_____

_____

_____

_____

4
CHAPTER

CLARITY

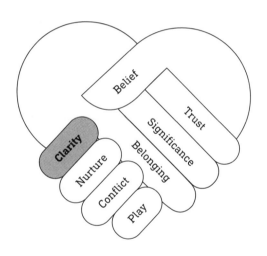

CLARITY
SAME BOAT AND SAME DIRECTION

As an educator, do you ever feel like you are in a boat all by yourself? You look around and all your colleagues are in their own boats, and everyone is rowing in different directions. It often feels like you are paddling upstream against the current.

You might feel like the district is constantly throwing new tasks or initiatives at you, creating a seemingly endless pile of to-dos. It's hard to figure out how it all fits together and why it's beneficial for the students and teachers. Maybe you feel like you're working against the system for the benefit of your students. Maybe there are things you want to do that you know will help your school or classroom, yet politics or time constraints make them impossible to accomplish.

All you can do is show up every day and do your best for your students, classroom, and school, but you're not sure you are doing the right things. Wouldn't it feel great to know what the "win" was? To have clarity of purpose and to know everything you did each day was taking you toward your individual and collective goals?

A college football team has similar dynamics as a school. They are large and ambiguous ecosystems that have many complexities. There are many passionate people who need to be put on the same boat and row in the same direction.

Dabo Swinney is one of the most successful college football coaches in America. His team at Clemson University has won two national championships, with promise to win more. He was hired as the head coach of Clemson in 2008. At his very emotional press conference upon being hired, he set the tone for his organization for years to come.

Dabo's goals were simple: 1) to bring in great student athletes, 2) to support them until they graduate, 3) to win championships, and 4) to send his players into the world better than they were when they arrived. At the time, Dabo was known for a slogan he often used: All in. It was a nonnegotiable, and every player he worked with was "all in."

In an interview with Hunter Renfrow, a receiver who had just caught the game-winning catch in the national championship game, the reporter asked what made Dabo a great coach. His response was, "Coach Swinney [serves] our hearts instead of our talents." Dabo never talked about stats. He talked about heart, about effort, about commitment to his team and the institution. If Hunter was "all in," Dabo knew Hunter would fulfill his potential and give the most back to Clemson.

Today, the words *all in* permeate the walls throughout the Clemson Athletic Association. Coach Swinney has managed to take the very complex process of coaching a football team into a set of clear goals and a single team mantra. Every coach and athlete who enters the program knows what success looks like, and they have a clear barometer on what the expectations are for them. When we create clarity, not only do we get everyone in the same boat, but we get them rowing in the same direction. And, if done well, with the current.

THE COURAGE OF CLARITY

Why It Is Hard

Clarity requires abundant communication and debate. Creating a shared vision and finding a common ground takes time, determination, and persistence. It's hard. It requires focus and intentionality to form clarity. Likewise, it takes vigilance to sustain and stay consistently true to a vision over the course of one or multiple years. It takes courage to stay the course and to continue to do the little things each and every day.

In any given year, there are a multitude of agendas within a school. Some are from your own team, some are pushed on you from the district, and some are mandated by the state and federal governments. There are new literacy initiatives, new state standards, safety regulations, technology requirements, redistricting, testing demands, and union demands ... among many other challenges.

On top of all this, there are new teachers who need to be supported, new students who need to be oriented, and new parents who need to be informed and comforted. The moment school starts, there is drama: difficult and disruptive students, disgruntled parents, and perhaps even dissention and disagreement among the team. It is so very difficult to build clarity within an environment that is so complex, dynamic, and ambiguous.

Before you know it, October comes, and you feel like you can finally lift your head up. Some things are going well, and others are not. Some initiatives never even got off the ground. The dreams of summer have become the realities of fall.

In January, everyone returns from break. It's a grind to get through testing to the end of the year. The mission and vision statement developed in August are forgotten. The chaos of the day-to-day routine forces us to take our eyes off what we defined at the beginning of the school year. What was clear has become blurred. We have become reactive rather than proactive.

To change culture, we must be very intentional about defining it. One of the greatest challenges of education is defining and building consensus on goals, objectives, core values, and shared practices that will unify us. If you are able to collaborate and do the work to build clarity, there is still another challenge in sustaining focus and attention on the vision throughout the year by continually communicating and reinforcing with all key stakeholders. It's a thousand acts of courage from day one to 180 and beyond.

CLARITY MATTERS

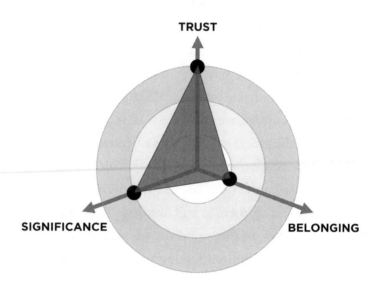

Courage Contribution

- Fostering **Clarity** will primarily drive **Trust**. When people share a common purpose, natural affinities develop, and motives are trusted.

- Secondarily, it will promote a sense of **Significance**. People are more productive when they align their goals and efforts to a clear and shared purpose.

- **Belonging** will be improved, connecting the team to a shared mission and vision.

You have to define the win. Everyone must know what success looks like and what their role is in contributing to the accomplishment of a collective goal. Without this, it's easy to simply become the sum of your parts.

Building collective clarity should be one of the first orders of business when creating a courageous school. Everyone must know what success looks like, they must understand how their job contributes to that success, and, perhaps most importantly, they must buy in. When we have found and agreed upon common vision, we are able to have constructive discussions and work together toward our shared goals.

What if you had clarity? You knew everything you were doing was aligned and supported everyone else in the building. You could take risks because the intent of your action was driving success for everyone. In the key moment, rather than pointing fingers, the team could now resolve any issues collectively and make adjustments to be better next time. How much more empowered would you be to innovate? How much better would you feel about your work when you went home? How much more efficient and effective would you be with your time?

It's intuitive that clarity is critical; no one disagrees as to its importance, yet it's elusive at most schools. If we don't have clarity, conflicting initiatives may arise, creative energy will be misguided, and frustration and disengagement will persist. This can lead to a lack of trust and community within your school, and you won't be able to progress efficiently.

Brené Brown is a leading researcher, author, and speaker on building authentic relationships. She has a phrase she shares in many of her books: "Clarity is kind." Clarity is not always comfortable or easy. It takes courage to give clarity when it may not be what someone wants to hear. But what is not kind is ambiguity. We owe it to our teams to give them the clear truths—even the ones that are unpopular or difficult.

When we don't have clarity, our best teachers and administrators become frustrated and confused. Their wonderful intentions and efforts may be misaligned or underappreciated. Likewise, lack of clarity is fertile ground for mediocrity. People become complacent without clarity of purpose. They're more susceptible to fall into ruts with no system in place to help get them back on track.

CLARITY IN ACTION

Ellen Cohan is a legendary educator and leadership coach in Georgia. She taught for twenty-one years and was an extremely successful principal and district leader for sixteen years. Her experience covered ten schools, and her influence has positively touched countless lives. Ellen had so much success that, upon retiring as a principal, districts around Georgia immediately reached out to her to help develop the next generation of leaders.

Her style is powerful. Her focus is to build clarity. She has an expression she asks every educator: "What is your California?" It alludes to the Gold Rush and the dream many pioneers had of finding gold and riches out West. In asking this, Ellen is asking educators to consider what they want to be remembered for. What is the most important thing to your classroom or school this year or over the span of your career? Her advice is for educators to find that one simple idea, that one thing they most hope will define their school. Asking these questions will help you and your team create absolute clarity on your "win."

This process was difficult for Mashburn Elementary. When Tracey and her team started, the school was underperforming, redistricting had created dramatic change, and the staff was unsure of how to approach the new learners in their building. Ellen's work with Tracey and the Mashburn team was painstaking. Defining Mashburn's California within such complexity was difficult. Together, the staff worked with the teachers to learn what they needed to be a thriving school. The entire team wanted the school to be a fun place that both teachers and students enjoyed. Over time, the school coined their California as "Make Today Ridiculously Amazing."

It's a high standard to have in education, but Mashburn was up for the challenge, even though they knew it could take some time to succeed. They decided to look at their school calendar a little differently. The question became how to make 180 days *ridiculously* amazing for kids and teachers. The staff knew that before they could even think about the learning, they would have to work on relationships with their students every day and turn little moments into memories. They gave input on changes that would brighten even the dullest day: fun music, painting the bathrooms, even simple things like adding filtered water machines throughout the building to promote drinking water.

The team also agreed on a framework designed to drive academic rigor within the ridiculously amazing culture. The process was supported by the statement "Watch your RERs," a play on "watching your backsides." Behind this clever statement was a very sophisticated process to transforming a school.

The first *R*, the ability to create *relationships* or meaningful connections with each other, students, and families was job one. It had to happen before the rest of the process could work. Once the foundational relationship was in place, educators could focus on creating student *engagement*, the *E*. This was all about implementation of effective instructional strategies and lesson plans.

The last *R*, for *rigor*, was the final step. Once the relationship was in place and the students were engaged in the learning process, the team was in a position to execute education with rigor. It was this rigor that drove the intentional outcomes defined by the learner profile mandated by the district.

Ultimately "Make Today Ridiculously Amazing" and "Watch Your RERs" were key to transforming the culture. Many referred to Mashburn Elementary as "Educational Disneyland." The staff and students followed the mantra, "Make Today Ridiculously Amazing," and they seemed to be able to do it each and every day. Amid all of this, achievement had gone up. In fact, the test scores were well above the expected score without ever making achievement a priority with the team. It was a multiyear journey to get there, and it wasn't an easy one, but the hard work and intentional focus on relationships, engagement and rigor had finally paid off.

GRADING YOURSELF ON CLARITY

Is clarity a strength in your school? Take this brief assessment individually or as a team to determine if everyone knows what the "win" is. The first five questions are designed to gauge the level of clarity you feel, while the last question will be your summary score that you can plot in the complete Assessment Tool provided in the Appendix.

Quiz Question (Circle the grade that applies)					
I clearly understand the critical goals and objectives of the school.	A	B	C	D	F
I believe in the focus and direction of the school.	A	B	C	D	F
I have a clear path for my role that aligns with the school's goals and objectives.	A	B	C	D	F
The goals and objectives of the school are effectively communicated and constantly reinforced.	A	B	C	D	F
The school's goals are directly aligned with the vision put forth by the district.	A	B	C	D	F
My overall Clarity Score is:	**A**	**B**	**C**	**D**	**F**

*Note: The online version of the full high-level assessment is provided free with this book at www.7mindsets.com/RAS. A school-wide Assessment Tool can be used school-wide by emailing info@7mindsets.com.

THE TIME IS NOW
Proven Practices to Start Building Clarity Today

Walk the Walk, Talk the Talk

In our workshops, we take schools through a process of defining their mission, vision, values, and rules of engagement. Many think back into the recesses of their minds and remember a mission or vision statement that might be posted somewhere on the wall or collecting dust in a closet. They are almost never able to recite any of it. And therein lies the problem.

Schools around the country are riddled with fantastic ideas that never get executed. Almost every school has some kind of mission and vision statement, and many have a set of values. Few can remember them, much less use them as guideposts for their work. Many times, they get caught under a pile of a thousand other things and rarely—if ever—get brought up after the ideas' initial conception. If teams do not intentionally bring the language into their everyday activity, it can quickly get forgotten.

If you buy into the importance of clarity—that school culture can be intentionally driven—then this is an essential ingredient to success. The truth is that any school could have high degrees of success with many different visions. It is really not the content of the message; it is the manner in which it is executed.

Put this messaging on walls, have it on recurring meeting agendas, and make T-shirts. More importantly, it needs to infiltrate the words you use each and every day. Constantly refer back to it and use it as the guidepost for how you operate and make decisions. When a team member has an idea, validate it against your California. Ask the team if this is aligned with getting you where you need to go. When you hire people and train them, make sure they're clear on the spirit of your organization and how they can support it and contribute to it. When people lose sight, kindly hold them accountable as a staff and help them grow to see how supporting the vision will make their school a better place.

Always Think and Communicate from the Inside Out

In his book *Start with Why*, Simon Sinek talks about communicating from the inside out. He uses the Golden Circle to illustrate the concept of Inside-Out Communication. It illustrates how most communication begins with what we do, then shifts to how we do it. And, as an afterthought, we might mention why we're doing it. When you communicate from the outside in, you lose the opportunity to connect your proposal to the shared intent of the organization. Rather than focusing on what needs to be done, start with why you are doing it.[15]

As you build clarity on what the "win" is (what your goals and objectives are), have it infiltrate the way you and your team communicate with one another. One way to really walk the walk is to continue to go back to the "why." Communicate from the inside out and think from the inside out as well. For example, when your "win" is creating relationships first with peers, students, and families in your building, it changes the way conversations are

---

[15] Sinek, *Start with Why*.

held. They shift focus from being centered around you to those around you.

Create Your Sentence

John F. Kennedy is famous for a sentence from his speech at Rice University in 1962: "We choose to go to the moon." It was a massive goal at the time, and seemingly impossible. But it gave a clear vision for the many men and women responsible for making it a reality.

When Kennedy visited NASA, he met with different workers around the facility. In one famous exchange he came across a janitor mopping the floors. He shook the man's hand and asked him what he did at NASA. The man smiled and responded, "I'm helping put a man on the moon."[16] The clarity of Kennedy's vision had permeated throughout NASA and into the work and spirit of every employee.

Have every team member write down their "sentence." If they want to be remembered for one thing this year, what would it be? Everyone should make sure that their sentence directly ties back to the goals of the school and the district. It allows us to focus our efforts, know that our work is congruent with the rest of the school, and know when we have been successful. This aligned likeness of intent is a major source of trust in a large complex organization such as a school.

Some examples of such sentences are:

- Empower every child to create a life they can be proud of.
- Believe in every student and work to get them to believe in themselves.

---

[16] Nemo, "NASA."

60

- I want every student to know I believe in them.
- Create a trusting environment where every student can thrive.
- Love them, teach them, and change the trajectory of their lives.
- I want to have at least one positive interaction with a different student every day this year.

Verbify or Verb It Up

Many schools have core values or underlying philosophies. Sometimes, even when we have the best intentions, these values might not be written out in an attention-grabbing way. This could be a big reason why these values and mission statements end up collecting dust somewhere. One way to make them more actionable is to "verbify" them into mantras. Rather than a core value of "Be engaging," verb it up to "*Make* every day ridiculously amazing!!!!!" Rather than "Believe in accountability," verbify it to "We *own* our results!!!!"

If you pay attention to sports teams, they use power statements or mantras very effectively. For example, Notre Dame has a sign that has been on the door of their locker room for generations that says, "Play Like a Champion Today." Every player touches the sign as a reminder before walking onto the field for a game. Mantras and fun sayings bring energy and give deeper meaning to what we're doing. They allow us to better reinforce and sustain efforts to build clarity. Find ways to build cultural power statements. It will go a long way in helping to build clarity and creating a culture that will sustain the mission and vision for years to come.

Together We Are Better

At one school we interviewed, the teachers told us the story of when their fifth-grade math state test scores had significantly dropped. The administration team partnered with the teachers for the answers. How could the scores be this bad? Together they dissected the scores down to the student level and by domain. This information turned out to be incredibly beneficial to them; the teachers knew exactly what they needed to change to better support the students' learning. It's not that the test is driving the teaching, but the teachers needed to know if they were teaching the standards and skills sufficiently. This allowed them to identify the problem and move forward together to progress as a team.

Getting everyone involved in critical decisions is key. Building consensus, finding common ground, and getting collective owner-ship on next steps is essential to solving problems and transform-ing culture. Whenever possible, involve others in the process of review, brainstorming, and defining solutions.

COMPANION GUIDE ACTIVITY: CREATING CLARITY

Clarity requires abundant communication and debate. Creating a shared vision and finding a common ground takes time, determination, and persistence. You must be intentional about defining your "win." Remember that sustaining clarity is a thousand acts of courage every single day.

Organization: What organizational changes or adjustments should be made (new roles or team structures)?

_____

_____

_____

_____

People: What professional development, book studies, and self-paced learning should be added?

_____

_____

_____

_____

Process: What activities can be added or integrated within the current schedule?

_____

_____

_____

_____

Technology and Tools: How can we leverage technology and tools?

_____

_____

_____

_____

5
CHAPTER

NURTURE

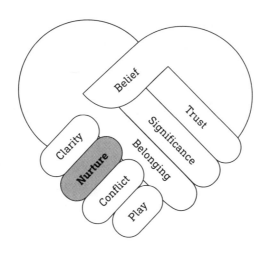

NURTURE
NATURE HOLDS THE ANSWERS

Like humans, plants are continually exposed to toxins. While humans fight environmental as well as social and emotional toxins, plants continually defend against new chemicals, gases, and changing environmental conditions. These elements can create stress and threaten the plants' health and even their existence.

Plants have developed detoxification processes to cleanse and to survive. Many times, however, environmental stressors overwhelm plants, causing death and sometimes even extinction. But life is powerful, and nature has devised an elegant approach, one rooted in community and connection.

Biologists at the University of California, Berkeley, have conducted some eye-opening research. In an effort to understand a plant's stress response to various kinds of toxins, they put plants in a closed container and introduced different contaminants in the form of chemicals and gases. They then observed the plants' responses.

While the plants were able to manage independently when introduced to a minor level of toxins, the release of a heavy dose of poisonous gas into the container would cause the plants to quickly wither and die. It was when the researchers decided to put multiple plants into a container that they could truly understand the power of connection.

When the gas was pumped into the container holding multiple plants, something very different happened: the plants evolved. They pulled different nutrients from the soil and metabolized differently. The community of plants began pumping out new forms of gases that actually detoxified the environment. Alone they could not survive, but together they thrived and transformed the very toxic environment that threatened them.[17]

Like the plants, our schools must often negotiate toxic environments. Anxiety, depression, and apathy permeate the hallways. Educators and students are experiencing trauma. Technology and social media are creating a whole host of new challenges that we seem ill-equipped to handle. These are issues that often seem to have no solutions.

It is our contention that there is a solution. It will come from the same place all solutions come from: our own hearts and minds. We must have the mindset that our role is bigger than our classroom, that we are critical to the collective. Our responsibilities do not stop at the doorway into our classroom or office. We must connect with and nurture everyone in the building, so we can all flourish collectively as well as individually.

We must feed and nurture one another. We must support each other and challenge one another to become better versions of ourselves, to feel excited, comfortable, and confident. If we can do this, just like the plants, we will pull new nutrients from the soil. We will breathe new gases and energy into the environment, so we not only survive but thrive and transform the toxicity that threatens us.

We only have so much time in a day. We can only work so hard and so smart. It is only if we learn to work with, for, and through one another that we can make our lives exponential and accomplish things that will transcend us.

---

[17] Ginwright, "Hope & Healing Keynote."

67

THE COURAGE OF NURTURE

Why It Is Hard

It seems easy to say that we would all be happier if we had each other's backs more and if we built bridges instead of walls with those with whom we have differences.

So why are we not supporting each other more? Why aren't we taking a greater vested interest in our colleagues? Why are we allowing dissention to be the sublime saboteur of a great school?

One reason is a narrow perspective on our roles. Many of us see our world contained by the four walls of our classroom. We don't appreciate our impact on every other teacher and student in the school, that our words and actions matter in a much broader context than with our students in our classroom. We call it the "I'm just a teacher" complex. We have been conditioned to think of our roles far too narrowly. It can also be scary to take greater levels of ownership. Being given responsibility feels great until we understand that we are accountable and that we may experience struggle and disappointment in the process. It's exciting to be part of a team selecting a new curriculum but not so much fun when the rollout falters and people start complaining.

Another reason is that nurturing ourselves and others is *hard*. It's like trying to get yourself to take that early morning run. You know you will feel great all day, but you're also tempted to stay in the comfort of your bed. It's like writing that thank you note, getting a physical, or seeing a therapist. It's hard in the moment, and

NURTURE

there may not be any real short-term consequences or gratification for the effort. The problem is that the accumulated neglect takes its toll and eventually it catches up to you.

Nurturing takes intentionality. It takes patience and the fortitude to build a connection with others no matter how difficult that may be or regardless of whether or not you get along with a coworker's personality. Likewise, it's hard to be kindly constructive with someone, to push them to their very best. It's much easier to comfort and support someone than to comfort and challenge them, but when there is challenge involved is often when people need us the most. Moreover, there is so much that needs to be done and so many fires that need to be put out. There is conflict and disagreement. It can be nearly impossible to slow down during the chaos and care for ourselves, much less our colleagues. The problem is that if we don't do the preventative maintenance with ourselves and each other, we eventually won't be able to deal with the bumps in the road, and our engines will overheat.

NURTURE MATTERS

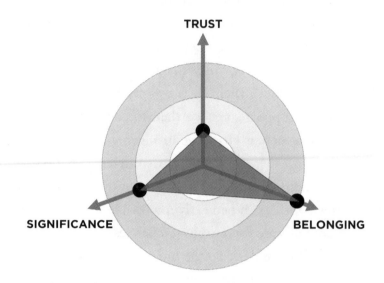

Courage Contribution

- Fostering **Nurture** will primarily drive **Belonging**. It provides support and makes team members accountable for other's growth.

- Secondarily, it will promote a sense of **Significance**. We feel more valued when we are valued more and supported by others.

- **Trust** will be improved through supportive actions and personal and collective accountability.

Nurture is the intersection of compassion and construction. It's about taking care of each other while firmly challenging one another. It's having each other's backs as well as a willingness to pour into one another and make investments in each other.

A nurturing environment has two critical components. It lets everyone know that they are supported, that we have their backs. It also firmly challenges each of us to foster individual and collective growth, knowing that one person's growth improves us all. It requires that we see ourselves as part of the collective whole, that we have a role in everything that happens in the school, and that when one person wins, we all win.

A typical school today is a complex, highly dynamic, and ambiguous ship. So many decisions and actions have to be taken every day for the educators and students to thrive. The leadership styles and organizational structures of the past often haven't met the needs of such diverse scenarios. The only way to truly be excellent in education is to tap into the creativity, innovation, and leadership of every single person in the building.

For that to happen, they need to be nurtured. They need to be taken care of when they need help, but they also need to be empowered and supported when they need a little push. And that can't just be the responsibility of the administrative team. It has to be the role and responsibility of every single one of us in the building. The days of hiding inside the friendly confines of your classroom are no more. We can't hide behind the "I'm just a teacher" complex anymore.

Imagine an environment where people understood you, where they knew about what was going on in your life outside of work. They asked you questions that were not ambiguous like, "How are you doing?" but rather questions like, "How did it go with the doctor yesterday?" or "How did your son do on his entrance exam?" Imagine you recently had a death in your family. Rather than simply walking past you, a colleague sees the struggle in your eyes. In that critical moment, they stop what they're doing and give their full attention to you, to simply listen and be available. How much more would we like coming to work if we knew people had our backs?

Nurture allows us to create a culture of *co-opetition*, a concept that combines cooperation with competition. In co-opetition, healthy competition fosters growth and excellence collectively. A competitive spirit can be healthy, but only when it nurtures and brings out the best in each other. Education can be a very competitive and cutthroat profession. We constantly compare ourselves to each other, and that is so harmful. In many ways, it's the opposite of self-compassion, and it creates disagreements, resentments, and disconnection. It makes work a chore, sucks out the joy, depletes our energy, and minimizes our ability to impact students.

Now consider an environment that has big dreams and high expectations. There is a healthy competition that is joyful and brings out the best in us. It is not about being better than someone else, it is about being our best and getting our teammates to be their very best. We push each other and we challenge one another but in the context of being on the same team. How much more liberated would you be to pursue personal and professional growth? How much more likely would you and your colleagues be to fulfill their potential?

By fostering a nurturing environment, we can create a culture in which we do push everyone in our organization to be their best. Nurture is such a powerful word because there is a kindness to it as well as a firmness. It is a concept filled with compassion and growth-mindedness. We want our team to take care of each other, but it is also essential that we all become better because of one another. We must collectively take ownership of each other and every student in the building.

The social and emotional health of our teachers and administrators is so critical. We are already part of the most anxious, medicated, obese, and addicted generation in our history. We are struggling just to get through the day, and we cannot model for our students what we do not have. We feel more cut off and alone—perhaps more than people ever have at any other time in our history. Apathy and disengagement are becoming the great epidemics of our day.

The antidote to disengagement is connection. When we connect with each other, we feel better and perform and function at higher levels. The way we nurture the adults in our building is by pouring into them, by getting to know them at a personal level, and by fostering the empathy and compassion that are the sources of courage and authenticity.

NURTURE IN ACTION

Sharing our story both heals us and connects us. Sarah Von Esh, the principal at Settles Bridge Elementary, used storytelling to create a greater sense of belonging in her team. At the end of staff meetings, she left time for teachers to share one good thing happening in their lives. She would ask for volunteers, and the room would go silent. She would sit and wait patiently, an act of courage in itself. Sarah said this was a place that she needed to lead. She would model what it looked like to share and be appropriately vulnerable.

It took time for teachers to open up. It turns out that at first, they felt like they were bragging about themselves. This changed when the staff started sharing. One would talk about how they just got their son potty-trained and then joke about the year-long struggle. It turned out other staff members had experienced this, or were in the process, and immediately had a connection. They now knew something meaningful about one another, something that connected them and made them more human to each other.

Sarah had one teacher share that her mom had been diagnosed with cancer last year. She had lost her hair and, for the first time, was allowing her granddaughter, the teacher's daughter, to see her without her wig. It was personal and powerful, and it connected Sarah's teachers to one another. One of the best ways to build courageous relationships is to give people a window into each other's soul. Sarah had allowed her teachers to see the kinder and gentler sides of each other—the parts that were flawed, human, and really likeable. This is the foundation for creating a ridiculously amazing school.

Storytelling is an excellent way to foster nurture among educators. All schools need to make sure they are building a sense of community with their staff. Take time to find ways for your team to get to know each other, to see the human side of one another, and to understand that you are all taking this challenging journey together.

GRADING YOURSELF

Is nurture a strength in your school? Take this brief assessment individually or as a team to determine if you and your team are taking a vested interest in each other. The first five questions are designed to gauge the level of nurture you feel, while the last question will be your summary score that you can plot in the complete Assessment Tool provided in the Appendix.

Quiz Question (Circle the grade that applies)

We are supportive and take care of one another.	A B C D F
I feel respected and appreciated.	A B C D F
When I am having a bad day, others pick me up.	A B C D F
I am challenged to grow personally and professionally.	A B C D F
There are informal and formal support structures to support me and help me develop.	A B C D F
My overall Nurture Score is:	**A B C D F**

Note: The online version of the full high-level assessment is provided free with this book at www.7mindsets.com/RAS. A school-wide Assessment Tool can be used school-wide by emailing info@7mindsets.com.

THE TIME IS NOW
Proven Practices to Start Building Nurture Today

Create Partnerships in Growth

One strategy effective goal-setters use is having an accountability partner. Team members pair up and form small groups. They discuss and share their personal and professional goals. As you work toward goals, it's important to have someone to talk with, someone who can look at your situation objectively and assist with adjustments and critical decisions.

Find someone or a small group on your team to partner with. Share your personal and professional goals and meet monthly to review progress. When you meet, talk about what you have accomplished, what your current focus is, and what the challenges are. This can be a critical part of ensuring we are growing individually and collectively and that we are taking a vested interest in each other's growth.

This small group dynamic fosters attitudes and environments where colleagues can build powerful relationships that support each other and hold one another accountable for personal and professional growth.

Perform Daily Random Acts of Nurture

One of the best ways to build or deepen a relationship is to make an investment by pouring into someone else. It could be a simple compliment, a note or text of support, helping them deal with a personal matter, or covering for them while they address an issue.

We have all heard of random acts of kindness. Take this to the next level by asking everyone on the team to do one thing every day for a colleague. Challenge them to not only perform acts of kindness but also acts that inspire and challenge their colleagues to grow and expand personally and professionally.

The goal should be to help out a different person each day. By the end of the year, each person should have done something for every faculty and staff member in the building. Make a contest of it. Make it part of your culture.

Make It Personal

Sarah Von Esh created intentional time within staff meetings to foster greater personal understanding of each other. Find time within your meeting structure for educators to share what is going on in their personal lives. Use personal storytelling as a tool to create courageous relationships within your school.

Initially, people may be hesitant to share but, if persistent, you can make this a powerful and positive influence on your team. When team members gain a deeper understanding of each other, it fosters empathy and compassion. It also allows team members to find commonalities and make deeper connections. This deeper understanding creates empathy, increases compassion, and deepens relationships significantly.

Create Empowered Teams

Deedee Westbrook has been the principal at Mid-Carolina Middle School for eleven years. She is a courageous leader, and her school was nominated in 2018 as one of Palmetto's Best—one of nine schools nominated in South Carolina.

Early in her career, Deedee learned the importance of nurturing. She had an extremely outgoing personality and she had to learn that while there are many benefits to being so relational, sometimes what others needed was for her to simply sit back and listen, learn, and build relationships. In her first year as a principal, a mentor had given her that advice, and she says it's the best advice she's ever received. She spent time observing her team rather than jumping in and immediately making changes. She quickly realized that the biggest challenge her school faced was the barriers her teachers had put up among themselves. They were not cohesive as a team, so many did not feel supported.

One thing she was able to do effectively was formalize a middle school teaming structure. The idea was to provide formal support structures for every teacher to get assistance, kind of like a first line of defense. One of the first questions she asked when she was approached by a teacher with a problem was whether they had discussed it with their team. The goal was to foster courage and vulnerability, to provide teachers with a platform to support one another, challenge each other, and promote collective innovation for the students. She sees the formation of this structure as a defining moment in her career, when she truly made herself exponential through her teachers.

As a team, it is important to figure out multiple levels of support. Educators face so many challenges and drama, and many realize there is absolutely no way they can always be the eye of the storm. They must get help. Build into your organizational structure an order that promotes and fosters nurture, facilitates a desire in each educator to get support, and makes them better and stronger through others.

Perform "Live to Give" Projects

A number of schools execute staff service projects prior to the start of the school year. Often, they raise money to create care packages for students from disadvantaged backgrounds. Each family might get a bag filled with notebooks, pencils, and other items needed for the school year. Others collaborate with the students to raise money for our troops.

Doing something for others, especially those in need in our community, brings out the best in us. In fact, not only does it have a positive effect on us individually, but it brings us together around a common purposeful mission. When these schools debrief after service projects, people see the best in each other, and they tend to find deep and meaningful connections. It's a powerful bonding experience.

Executing staff service projects in the community fosters an environment of nurture. It says we take care of our community and we take care of each other so we can take care of our students and their families. It has an added benefit of making teachers proud of their school and the work it's doing.

Use Emotional Thermometers

It's important to understand that we all have challenges. Some days are great, and some days we struggle. It can be good to know when our team members are having a tough day, and one way to do this is a concept we have seen used called an Emotional Thermometer.

When in a large or small team meeting, ask everyone to rank their current emotional status on a scale of one to ten. At first, team members may be reserved to share how they're truly feeling, but over time, as nurture is created, this becomes a valuable tool of understanding and being there for one another. It also reinforces that it's okay to have bad days. It tells team members, "I have your back today because I know you will be there to pick me up one day when I need it in the future."

Share Successes

There is a Swedish proverb that teaches us, "Sorrow shared is halved, joy shared is doubled." If we give our team the opportunity to share what is working and what they are proud of, it can have powerful benefits. It allows us to provide others the opportunity to learn and grow from our experiences. It can help mitigate the unhealthy competitive forces that sometimes exist among educators. Finally, it can be affirming and help teachers feel a greater feeling of accomplishment and significance.

COMPANION GUIDE ACTIVITY: FOSTERING NURTURE

A nurturing environment has two critical components. First, it lets everyone know that they are supported, that we have their backs. Second, it firmly challenges each of us to foster individual and collective growth, knowing that one person's growth improves us all. It requires that we see ourselves as part of the collective whole, that we have a role in everything that happens in the school, and that when one person wins, we all win.

Organization: What organizational changes or adjustments should be made (new roles or team structures)?

_____

_____

_____

_____

People: What professional development, book studies, and self-paced learning should be added?

_____

_____

_____

_____

Process: What activities can be added or integrated within the current schedule?

_____

_____

_____

_____

Technology and Tools: How can we leverage technology and tools?

_____

_____

_____

_____

6
CHAPTER

CONFLICT

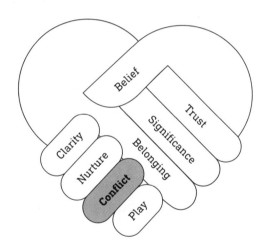

CONFLICT
FORGING RELATIONSHIPS THROUGH CONFLICT

Iron in its natural state is not a very strong substance on its own. In fact, it would be described as brittle. However, it is the primary ingredient for steel, one of the strongest materials known to man. In a process perfected by ancient Japanese swordsmiths for the samurai, we learned iron could become high-quality steel only after going through an adverse process of being forged and folded.

When iron is forged, it is heated to very high temperatures (up to 1150°C or 2102°F), hammered, and then cooled. The process of folding the substance into itself increases its strength. In ancient times, as well as in modern Japanese sword-making, the iron goes through ten to fifteen rounds of folding.[18] As all this occurs, steel—an alloy of iron—is created. The iron has been fundamentally transformed into one of the most cost-effective, durable, and strongest substances in the world. Japanese swordsmiths were able to create some of the strongest and sharpest blades ever known to man. It was only through the introduction of extreme circumstances that the iron could fulfill its potential.

Many times, the very situation that creates the greatest discomfort is most essential to success. Like iron, our ability to use adversity in constructive ways can strengthen and unify us. It is through adversity that we can come together, grow, and sharpen

---

[18] University of Oslo, "Bog Iron."

our impact. Ironically, going through conflict is a primary source of trust in our organization. How we handle conflict largely dictates whether trust is a strength or weakness for us.

THE COURAGE OF CONFLICT

Why It Is Hard

The vast majority of us avoid conflict. Engaging in conflict doesn't feel good. It makes us uncomfortable. We also have concern for hurting others or hurting our relationships with them. We have all seen colleagues who aggressively confront others, and it isn't very productive. Even effective discourse can make situations uncomfortable, and the benefits are often not immediately visible.

Now, put this fear of conflict into an educational setting. Any day in a school is unique—you never quite know what will happen. In the mornings, you are either greeting students at your classroom or you are working in some capacity to help get students into the school doors. During the day, it's teaching, returning phone calls, checking email, planning, and putting out the fires of the day.

You are tired and worn down and may not be emotionally ready to deal with challenge. Conflict can sneak up on you or it can hit you fast and furious. When your day is already rushed, it's especially difficult to take the time to slow down and think about how something should be handled. When you factor in different personality types, it can get even more complicated.

So why take the risk of causing more trouble, of damaging an already strained relationship, when you can just do nothing? You do it because not doing something means complacency. In schools, you are either growing or you are withering. The key to ensuring constant growth is a mindset that understands conflict and challenge which, when effectively executed, is a sign of true health and vitality within an organization.

We must find ways to make healthy discourse part of our culture. We must learn to disagree agreeably. If we do not, differences will sabotage our efforts to become a great school and it will become a "death by a thousand papercuts" scenario. We must find and cultivate the courage to face challenges constructively and respectfully.

CONFLICT MATTERS

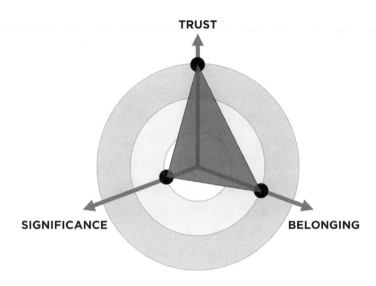

TRUST

SIGNIFICANCE

BELONGING

Courage Contribution

- Fostering **Conflict** will primarily drive **Trust**. Healthy discourse is the catalyst of strong relationships that grow together through challenge.

- Secondarily, it will promote a sense of **Belonging**. Teachers connect more deeply when they are comfortable talking things out with colleagues.

- **Significance** will be improved as constructive debate builds competence and drives creativity and innovation.

We should get excited by the problems and the challenges. It may not be fast or easy, but sometimes we learn the most along the path of addressing obstacles, which leads us to the greatest improvement in the end.

We all have a relationship with conflict. Some of us actually enjoy it. We see it as part of the process. It heightens our focus and energy. These people can be movers and shakers; they make things happen and they push us to be better. But sometimes "conflict enjoyers" can be like bulls in a china shop. We jump head in with very little empathy, and conflict becomes a source of animosity and dissention.

Some of us dodge conflict like the plague. We are "conflict avoiders." We are powerful in our empathy and understanding. When we speak up, we can be very effective. Unfortunately, sometimes we worry—perhaps too much—about other people's feelings and our relationships with them. We don't want to ruffle feathers or rock the boat. But being so cautious can mean that the problems don't actually go away or get resolved. If we don't deal with the problems, they fester and grow, ultimately causing more damage than if they had been discussed in the first place.

Whether you are a "conflict enjoyer" or "conflict avoider," the reality is that conflict is inevitable. We need to face conflict head-on but with empathy and compassion for all involved. When we address conflict openly, we can move forward constructively.

Just like the best time to show courage is in the presence of fear, the best time to build trusting relationships is in the presence of challenge. Great marriages are strengthened by their trials. We find out who our true friends are in our darkest hours. The relationships soldiers who have fought side-by-side are among the strongest and most loyal we see. Challenge is the path to building relationships. Our perspectives and approaches toward discourse largely dictate the trust and respect that is built within our team.

Imagine you are co-teaching a class. The other teacher does or says something that you are uncomfortable with. In this moment, rather than simply forgetting about it, you naturally and easily approach the colleague with your concern. He does not get offended, but rather respects what you are saying and truly reflects on his actions. Imagine, as a principal, seeing teachers addressing their issues directly. You do not get caught up in destructive drama, but rather issues get resolved positively and constructively throughout the classrooms and hallways. And when teachers have problems with you, they do not fester. In a courageous moment, they come to you and talk it out before it sabotages the work everyone is focused on with the students. How much more empowered would you feel? How much more effective do you think you and your team would be?

Not only is adversity the path to trust, it is also a primary catalyst for creativity and innovation within an organization. Healthy constructive debate stirs our emotions, heightens our intensity, and forces us to look at things differently. When we would ask educators to define the most important moment in their career, they almost always pointed to a moment or situation of great challenge when they learned a lesson, developed a perspective, or built great trust with their colleagues. The challenges are the path and the obstacles are the way. As Jeff once heard John Lasseter, CEO of Pixar, say at a LeaderCast event, "Problems are not impediments to the job, they are the job."

CONFLICT IN ACTION

Beth Hench, the Principal at Ayersville Elementary School in Ohio, described to us the turning point in her career. It was her best and worst day as an educator. She was a new principal with strong convictions. Knowing that for the previous several years, most of the staff professional development revolved around changes in state mandates, she had come into the position strong, wanting to make some significant changes. She had decided to push into the school an inclusion-style co-teaching model for their special needs population. She had gotten buy-in from the special education department and great enthusiasm from the parents. What she had not thought to do was ask for feedback from her general education teachers.

At that time, Beth was also making promises of changes to come; she wanted to do away with the elementary building tracking entire grade levels into high, middle, and low classrooms. She wanted to see small group instruction implemented in classrooms across grade levels and content areas. She wanted to see teachers using data to drive the instruction in their classrooms. The problem was, historically, the school had performed well, and teachers had not been asked to make instructional changes as long as it continued to do so. Additionally, Beth can admit now that she did not take time to clearly and specifically share her vision with the staff and build enough rapport for them to trust that she was making decisions based on what was best for students and staff.

It all came to a head one November afternoon while Beth was dealing with a suspension. While the student's mother was sitting in the lobby, more than a dozen teachers walked into Beth's office, expressed their frustration with changes that she was making, and asked to meet. Blindsided, she asked the teachers for some time, finished the suspension conversation, and went home in tears, believing she had made a catastrophic mistake. She was frustrated, tired, and had one of the hardest nights of her career.

Challenge and conflict are inevitable. They can and must happen in the best of schools. Passionate people are working hard to do what is best for the students. This creates pressure points that cause tension. How we deal with this pressure will determine whether challenge is a source of innovation or decay within our school.

Beth realized she had burned some bridges with her teachers. She called her superintendent, shared her situation, and said she had to find a way to build rapport with her teachers while still continuing to improve instruction. She knew her school needed significant change but had isolated herself and was going about it the wrong way. That same day, Beth met with her assistant principal, and together they conceptualized a two-pronged professional development plan focusing on culture and instruction. The plan asked volunteers to visit the Ron Clark Academy, a revolutionary school in Atlanta, Georgia, that models innovative practices for educators. Additionally, they observed courageous schools around the country. Collectively they wanted to see what was possible— both culturally and instructionally—and then create a plan to get there together.

It took nearly three years to empower every staff member through these visits. As each group of staff took the trip to

Georgia, they were asked to return to school, reflect, and share their experiences with others. Every group brought back a unique perspective on what they had learned, and was able to build upon at least one area that made an impression on them while on the trip. Some teachers focused on something as simple as teaching students manners. Some teachers were impacted by classroom transformations and dove into creating experiences, not just lessons, for students. Many teachers were influenced by the teaching styles they saw when visiting other high-performing classrooms and vowed to make changes within their own rooms: from number talks to small-group teaching to making data-informed decisions, teachers began to see ways to grow their own instructional strategies.

A great amount of instructional and cultural change became evident through the two-pronged professional development focus. Throughout the process, though, many tough conversations were had. Teachers were challenged in their thinking. Beth was challenged in her own thinking. They were pushed to have conversations that would have never been possible if the initial struggles hadn't occurred.

Since that afternoon in November, Beth's elementary school, students, and staff have grown tremendously. A building-wide Multi-Tiered System of Supports (MTSS) program has been implemented to help build foundational skills in reading and improve state test scores. A building leadership team has been created and tasked with continuing to tweak current programs and find additional ways to do what's best for kids. There have been many twists and turns and ups and downs on this journey, but Beth's staff is now moving in the same direction—together.

GRADING YOURSELF

Is dealing with conflict a strength in your school? Take this brief assessment individually or as a team to determine if your school has a healthy relationship with conflict. The first five questions are designed to gauge the level of healthy conflict you feel, while the last question will be your summary score that you can plot in the complete Assessment Tool provided in the Appendix.

Quiz Question (Circle the grade that applies)	
Our school is good about not gossiping or talking negatively behind each other's backs.	A B C D F
I am comfortable approaching leadership with difficult conversations.	A B C D F
Our team members are skilled at non-defensive communication (e.g., they don't make it personal or take it personally).	A B C D F
I can have a healthy debate with a colleague without feelings getting hurt.	A B C D F
Our team faces our biggest challenges head-on.	A B C D F
My overall Conflict Score is:	**A B C D F**

Note: The online version of the full high-level assessment is provided free with this book at www.7mindsets.com/RAS. A school-wide Assessment Tool can be used school-wide by emailing info@7mindsets.com.

THE TIME IS NOW
Proven Practices to Start Building Healthy Conflict Today

What's Your Personality?

There are a myriad of personality tests available. If you haven't already, take one individually and as a team. It can be very eye-opening to gain a better understanding of yourself and build an appreciation for the strengths and assets you bring to the table. It's also very powerful when your team builds a broader understanding of the different personalities, strengths, and weaknesses that each team member brings to the table.

This understanding fosters greater empathy and compassion. When done well, it creates appreciation and respect for others' strengths and builds better collaboration and innovation within your organization.

Always Talk It Out

Often, what is not said causes the most damage. Disagreements and dissention do not go away. If not faced head-on, they will grow and fester.

Make one of your core values about healthy conflict. Verbify it into a mantra like, "We always talk it out." The idea is to create a dynamic where everyone can find the courage and strength to disagree and engage in constructive dialogue with each other for the benefit of the students.

Effective conflict is the catalyst for creating truly strong bonds. It is also the source of creativity and innovation, as constructive discourse allows people to find better solutions together. This mindset needs to be fostered among the team and then executed in the way you operate as a staff. Make constructive discourse a value or part of the ethos of your school.

Every Door Is Open

We've observed that schools with courageous relationships almost always have an open-door policy. It was very common for educators we interviewed to exclaim how wonderful it was to work in an environment where, if they had a problem, they felt comfortable approaching colleagues whether they were teachers or administrators.

The hidden frustrations and disagreements are toxic to great teams. We have to get them out in the open. It is important that we make constructive dialogue the expectation and the norm; it should be celebrated! Essential to doing this is making sure every team member is approachable. Everyone's door must be open. Very few things are more important than a critical conversation with a team member. These are the crucial moments, and when approached, we need to become present and fully engage in the dialogue with our colleagues.

Find Out How You Deal with Conflict

There are tools that help us understand how we specifically deal with conflict. This can be powerful information in understanding if you are a "conflict enjoyer" or a "conflict avoider." This understanding can help all of us move toward engaging in healthy conflict in a way that takes us forward and does not create divisiveness.

This information can also be powerful to our team. If we know someone is very uncomfortable with conflict, we can find ways to make sure their voice is heard and bring out more of their constructive thinking. Likewise, if we have colleagues who are very comfortable with conflict, it gives us great perspective on how to hear better what they are saying and not let what they say ruffle our feathers.

Don't Take It Personally, Don't Make It Personal

In his book *Overcoming the Five Dysfunctions of a Team*, Patrick Lencioni talks about the mastering conflict and the conflict continuum. Central to this philosophy is refining your organization's ability to always have healthy discourse.[19] The most destructive deterrent of healthy debate is your team members' inability to keep the discussion constructive and not make or take things personally.

There are many things we do that make it very difficult to have a high-quality debate. It's part what we say, it's part how we say it, and a lot of it has to do with our body language. There are techniques that can help all of us handle ourselves better in difficult conversations.

We need to give our team the comfort and confidence to approach colleagues and present ideas in impersonal and unthreatening ways. Likewise, by creating a culture of constructive discourse, we facilitate a mindset that this is just part of the process; it is not personal, it is about doing what is right for every student.

Investments made in professional development in these areas may just be some of the best money your school spends. Make it

---

[19] Lencioni, *Dysfunctions*, 37–41.

a priority and understand its importance. Find classes on Non-Defensive Communication or other practices that will allow your team to embrace the uncomfortable conversations and work collaboratively and creatively to innovate and solve the challenges they face.

Agree to Disagree, Agreeably

We must learn to be comfortable with conflict. We also need a mindset of constructive discourse. A great ground rule for a meeting or a culture is to "agree to disagree agreeably." This perspective does three things: First, it sets the expectation that we can and should disagree. This is actually healthy to creativity and innovation. Secondly, it sets the expectation that we will have healthy debate, but we will refrain from anger, frustration, or making things personal. Finally, there is a hidden benefit in that everyone is set up to leave the debate in the room and to move forward collectively and unified in the direction of whatever decisions were made.

Create a Culture of Discomfort

As we interviewed teachers, we consistently heard how wonderful it was to work at a school where you could disagree agreeably—where educators could positively confront one another, colleagues would not get defensive, and discussion and collaboration would cnsue.

When people can disagree with each other and lobby for different ideas, your organization is healthier. Disagreements often result in a more thorough study of options and better decisions and direction. In his book *The Empowered Manager*, Peter Block argues that an unwillingness to participate in organizational conflict will prevent any organization from accomplishing its goals.[20]

If the vision for your school is clear, if everyone is on the same page and agrees on what success looks like, then they must have the courage to express disagreement and participate in healthy debate. Every great school should have a value or ethos statement that drives people to talk things out, resolve differences, and co-create better solutions together. At Mashburn, another of their ethos statements is "Together We Are Better." Challenge and collaboration should be promoted, modeled, and celebrated as essential to success.

---

[20] Block, *Manager*, 7–8.

COMPANION GUIDE ACTIVITY:
BUILDING CONSTRUCTIVE CONFLICT

Healthy conflict is an essential part of the growth process. It takes courage to allow conflicts to build relationships, rather than tear them down. Knowing how you handle conflict is also important in dealing with issues when they come up. When we address conflict openly and when we can move forward constructively, it becomes a catalyst for not only trust but creativity, innovation, and—ultimately—sustained excellence.

Organization: What organizational changes or adjustments should be made (new roles or team structures)?

_____

_____

_____

_____

People: What professional development, book studies, and self-paced learning should be added?

_____

_____

_____

_____

Process: What activities can be added or integrated within the current schedule?

_____

_____

_____

_____

Technology and Tools: How can we leverage technology and tools?

_____

_____

_____

_____

PLAY

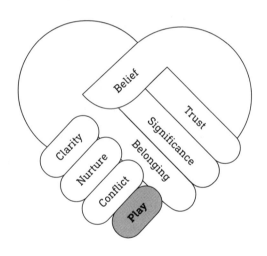

PLAY
THE VIBE

Stuart Brown is a leading expert on play. In his book *Play: How It Shapes the Brain, Opens the Imagination, and Invigorates the Soul*, he shares a story of some huskies playing on the frozen tundra just north of Churchill, Manitoba, in November. They were playing in the ice when a 1,200-pound male polar bear approached. Very wild and very hungry, he crouched into his attack stance and assumed a predatory gaze. He was fixed on the huskies, and a photographer nearby knew the huskies were in trouble.

On the other side of that predatory gaze was a female husky in a playful bow, excitedly wagging her tail. Then something amazing happened. The very fixed aggressive behavior of the polar bear dissipated. The polar bear stood up over the husky, no claws or teeth extended, and the two animals began a beautiful and playful dance. It overrode the nature of the polar bear and created something beautiful. [21]

If you look at the photographs taken that day, you can see the two animals in an altered state, one of pure joy and enthusiasm. They are in a state of play.

That is the power of play. When introduced into intense environments, it can eliminate divisive circumstances. It can foster joy, connections, and relationships where animosity, anger, and divisiveness exist. It can change everything in an instant. It can make

[21] Brown, *Play*.

friends out of enemies and get us all to perform and function at higher levels.

Every now and then when we walk into a school, we notice it has what we call the Vibe. It is, simply put, electric. The teachers are laughing and joking with each other. The students are giving high fives to the school resource officer (SRO) and holding doors open for the teachers. Frequent eye contact is made and smiles are on almost everyone's faces. The school seems to have taken a life of its own—from the student work on the wall to the anticipation for the next sporting event, the excitement is infectious.

A school like this is that elusive "fun school." It is the school every teacher wants to work for, every parent wants their child to attend, and every student wants to be at. After years of observing schools, we have come to appreciate these precious rare environments but, even more, what we know has been done to create them. When we see this type of atmosphere, we truly treasure it because we understand what it takes to get there. It most likely started many years ago and always included a healthy dose of play. It is this spirit of play that breaks down walls, connects people deeply with one another, and opens up the possibility of giving your school that Vibe.

THE COURAGE OF PLAY

Why It Is Hard

For most of us, it is about the age of eleven or twelve that things change. We lose that sense of wonder, the innocence of our youth, and that unbridled enthusiasm we have to simply play. Do you remember in your own life when certain things lost their luster? That crazy excitement you would get about a friend coming over or going to a birthday party. The exhilaration of riding a bike or going to a pool, fair, or amusement park. That pure joy that was associated with just doing something, without any concern for outcomes.

As we mature, our brains change, and society conditions us. It teaches us to put away childish things, to grow up, and to take on responsibility. Our culture tends to discourage play. We see it as a distraction, as unproductive time that is disruptive to efficiency and effectiveness. Unfortunately for us as adults, play is often dismissed in everyday life and is viewed as immature, unproductive, and unwelcome.

Some companies have created a trend of transforming their work environment by incorporating play. Offering yoga classes, throwing regular birthday parties, or providing games such as ping pong, they have learned that play results in more work productivity, higher job satisfaction, increased morale, and a decrease in team absences and turnover.

While this can work in the corporate world where schedules are more flexible, it's much more difficult in the very rigid and structured school day, especially in high schools. Education is hard. There is a lot of seriousness, drama, and intensity. It's difficult to find ways to create joyful experiences among our team. Given the pressures and responsibilities of the education world, it can be tough to justify setting aside time to foster play. If team members have other important tasks already on their plates, they might reject activities like this that don't necessarily have a tangible or concrete outcome.

In *Play*, Stuart Brown suggests that deprivation of play has serious consequences. "You begin to see that the perseverance and joy in work is lessened and life is much more laborious," he concludes. Over time, we might get cranky, rigid, or feel stuck in a rut or victimized by life.[22] Teachers and staff who are unable to find joy at work will wither. They will disengage and possibly even lose their sense of purpose. We cannot afford to lose our spirit of play; we just need to think about how it looks in a professional setting.

---

[22] Brown, *Play*, 123–157.

PLAY MATTERS

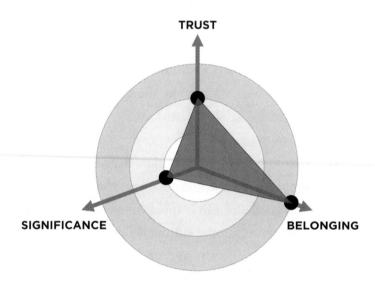

Courage Contribution

- Fostering **Play** will primarily drive **Belonging**. Informal play drives personal understanding and connections, which fosters deeper relationships and community.

- Secondarily, it will promote a sense of **Trust**. By fostering personal connections, deeper relationships emerge more rooted in trust.

- **Significance** will be improved by the natural benefits of **Play**, reducing stress, increasing creativity and mental functioning, as well as increasing energy and engagement levels.

We have to find a way to make school a place our educators want to be. It must be a place where they experience joy and that somehow enriches their lives in ways other than financially or professionally.

106

Play is any activity performed for self-amusement that has behavioral, social, and psychological rewards. It can be a stand-alone activity, like playing a game, or it can be integrated into non-play activities, like playing music during a carpool. It can be group-based, like watching a funny video together, or individual-based, like taking a vacation, reading a book, or exercising.

If you have ever worked out, you may have heard of a term called muscle confusion. Many times, when we get into a routine, the process of growth can slow, and we can become stagnate. When working out, if you do the same routine over and over again, your mind and body adjust and the pace of your improvement slows. Trainers will work with you to switch up your routine. They do this to confuse your muscles and make them work harder to adapt to changes in your routine.

Play is a way to create a form of this muscle confusion in the workplace. It keeps things fresh, changes things up, and keeps us on our toes. Play fosters engagement, creativity, and spontaneity. It fosters expanded opportunity to build relationships, experience joy, and create positive energy and enthusiasm. It promotes new opportunities to grow trust and foster a greater sense of belonging and significance among the team.

Play also allows us to relax, unwind, and regain our energy and enthusiasm. Our minds, bodies, and psyches are like engines. They can only go so fast and so far for so long. Play is preventative maintenance, but it is also an amplifier of our energy and effectiveness. It's a primary source for rejuvenating ourselves and tapping into our creative and productive energy. It also has massive impact collectively on education.

Schools that have that Vibe do not just happen. They are the cul-mination of a thousand little things that created the conditions where the magic can occur—where the relationships are in place, the students are engaged, and true education can be executed with rigor. That can't happen without play.

This might sound silly when you think about it, but schools with the Vibe have a nature where goofiness and fun—even cheesiness—are not only welcomed, they're encouraged. When there is a sense of play in a school, it's easier for everyone in the building to open up to activities that evoke joy, especially those where the experience of doing is often more important than any outcome. Still, the outcomes are ultimately profound.

Play isn't about the person who is outgoing, most social, or even the most popular. It isn't about getting on top of tables or being the loudest cheerleader. It's about creating moments of laughter and connection and pouring into one another through emotion. Play is about letting yourself loosen up to make those connections. Just like you connect with people who you go through hard situa-tions with, you also connect with people who you laugh with.

Play makes us better for others. It stimulates the mind, it pro-motes creativity, and, by reducing stress and depression, it makes us sharper and more focused. It gives us energy and enthusiasm to be present and engage more deeply with others. It creates environ-ments where you learn about others at a personal level. This drives a greater understanding of others, which promotes empathy and compassion.

Play is one of the most effective tools for keeping relationships exciting. It brings vitality and resilience to relationships, and it can heal resentments and divisiveness. It allows us to feel comfortable and safe with one another, and it builds ridiculously amazing relationships. These are the relationships that allow us to open up, to be vulnerable and truly maximize the meaning and productivity derived from our connections.

When we interviewed students about their favorite teacher or administrator, they would share stories—these were almost always rooted in play. A student shared with us about a physics teacher who would drop a watermelon off a twenty-foot deck to clarify some Newtonian Laws. One group of students most loved their school because teachers personalized greetings each morning when they entered the classroom. Another student who shared his most powerful memory in education was when his professor taught him physics at the local billiards hall. Many of the things we remember most—that have the greatest impact on us—are rooted in play.

Play in many ways is a primary source of engagement with students, but it must be fostered among the staff first before it can permeate the classrooms. The energy we create among ourselves is modeled and then presented to our students. More importantly, play is a primary conduit for building trust and creating a sense of belonging among our staff. Once this is developed among the team, these same conditions can be fostered in the classroom with our students.

PLAY IN ACTION

One test-taking season, Mashburn Elementary's teachers had an idea. They had done pep rallies in the past, but those had always been about test prep. "Let's get them ready; let's get them focused," had been the intent. The truth was the previous pep rallies were a little boring and didn't really work. The kids did not need to hear another person tell them to get a good night's sleep and be prepared for the tests.

This time they were going to do something different. The goal was to get the kids energized. The team at Mashburn wrote some new lyrics to Rachel Platten's hit "Fight Song." It went like this:

I'm a smart kid
Here at Mashburn
About to take a test,
The Georgia milestones

It is a simple test
Got my number 2
I'll read every word
And do my very best

And all those things I studied for
Strategies inside my brain
I will put them down today
They will hear my voice this time
I will rock this test
I am Mashburn strong

Prove I've got it song
My powers turn on
Starting right now
I'll be strong

This is my test song
it's gonna be great because
Everyone believes

I still got a lot of smarts left in me
Oh, I've still got a lot of smarts left in me

They wanted to give the kids their own fight song to rally around. Cori Moon, an incredibly talented singer at a local church and a Mashburn parent, sang and recorded the new song for the staff to use.

Then the magic of play took over. It was getting late in the day, and there were only three days until the testing pep rally where the video would be released. To film the video, the team grabbed their wigs and tutus and started lip-synching to the song while dancing down the hall. They took their best shot, and it turned out great. The only problem was the ending. It lacked pop.

They needed kids. They rounded up a few students, put them in wigs, and let them lip-synch the ending. Now that would be a big close and give the video just the pop it needed. The video was a huge success. When they pushed it out to the families, it went viral.

With the success of that video, the culture of video production grew. They did one at the end of the year. As the students came back the following August, another video was released. As momentum grew, the staff began to want more. The big idea hit to do a flash mob for the students at the next year's pep rally. The message in the flash mob was to "shake it off." Teachers wanted to communicate to students that when they took the test and a question stumped them, they should not worry but instead shake it off and know they are more than a test question.

These pep rallies became a huge tradition and had a bit of competitive edge to them. As teachers brainstormed how to make the next year's pep rally even more amazing for the students, the fifth graders decided they wanted to do a flash mob of their own to celebrate the teachers and administrators. They worked with the music teacher to create their own song and surprise everyone. It started with a very shy fifth grader interrupting Tracey during an assembly. He nervously interrupted by running onto the stage and telling her, "We've got something for you!" Then the student body erupted into a flash mob of its own. The teachers went wild as the students ended *their* pep rally with a tribute to their amazing teachers.

Experiences like this are those critical moments. They become our strongest memories and the experiences that largely define us. They can only happen if we have created the conditions for play. The videos at Mashburn were powerful because they connected the teachers to each other, they connected the teachers to the students, and they even connected the school more deeply to the community. The videos empowered the teachers and ultimately empowered the students. None of this would have happened without a strong culture of play.

GRADING YOURSELF

Is play a strength in your school? Take this brief assessment individually or as a team to determine if your school plays. The first five questions are designed to gauge the level of play you feel, while the last question will be your summary score that you can plot in the complete Assessment Tool provided in the Appendix.

Quiz Question (Circle the grade that applies)					
I am comfortable being myself around my colleagues.	A	B	C	D	F
I have fun at my school.	A	B	C	D	F
Time is created for me to play and connect with colleagues in informal settings.	A	B	C	D	F
I have time to decompress and rejuvenate myself appropriately.	A	B	C	D	F
I enjoy being with my colleagues.	A	B	C	D	F
My overall Play Score is:	**A**	**B**	**C**	**D**	**F**

Note: The online version of the full high-level assessment is provided free with this book at www.7mindsets.com/RAS. A school-wide Assessment Tool can be used school-wide by emailing info@7mindsets.com.

THE TIME IS NOW
Proven Practices to Start Building Play Today

Make It Musical

There are many benefits to listening to music. It makes us happier, enhances our energy and physical performance, lowers stress, reduces depression, strengthens learning and memory, and helps us to relax.[23] Whenever possible, find opportunities to play music in the school's hallways, classrooms, and conference rooms. Have fun with it. Let different students and staff choose the music and share one another's culture. Identify DJs of the week, and make it part of everything you do.

Music is a form of personal expression. It deepens our understanding of one another and creates deeper connection with others. It fosters understanding, which ultimately builds trust. Likewise, music creates joy. It makes work more interesting and fun, which fosters greater connection among the team.

Invest in You!

While the old saying is that if you find your passion, you won't work a day in your life, that's actually not true. When you are doing your passion, you can feel even more tempted to overwork, which can lead to burnout and stress. Keep certain times completely free of school—build in time for friends, exercise, and family that is free of technology and school thoughts. Another idea is

---

[23] Chappel, "Scientists."

to change out of your work clothes when you get home so you can separate yourself from the thoughts of your workday. All educators bring emotional (and physical) work home with them each night. We need to take a break from the worry of the students and the pressures of the job. Space gives us great perspective!

Turn 180 Days into 180 Memories

When you take the number of days you are together or have students (whether it's 180, 170, or 165), we must find a way to make each day special. Research shows that when we connect a feeling to emotion, smell, or music, it's more memorable and we retain what we have learned better.[24] You can connect these days to a fun calendar to celebrate pretty much anything you want or need. Some schools do wacky days to support school spirit such as Passion First Day, Grilled Cheese Day, National Jelly Bean Day, World Kindness Day, National Joke Day, or National Compliment Day. We can also turn each day into an incredible memory just by celebrating each other.

Get Serious About Play

Create a committee whose job is to create play in the building for teachers. When teachers play, they turn around and play with their students. One school we interviewed created a program that focuses on a different fun activity every six weeks. Most were clue-based, and teachers would either get a clue through email or they would be hidden in the workroom. Teachers had to work together to solve the clues. There were fun prizes involved but, more importantly, lots of laughs. After each six-week game,

---

[24]Tyng, et al., "Emotion."

many of the teachers went back and created similar activities for their students.

Celebrate Special Events

For many people, the remembrance and recognition of special dates, such as their birthday or anniversary, is a precious act. Taking a little time on the morning announcements or during staff meetings can help team members feel appreciated. Have someone manage all the key personal dates of your team including birthdays, anniversaries, and years teaching. Find small ways to celebrate.

Dress It Up!

We heard a story of a teacher who, in her 20 years of experience, had never had any interest in dressing up for PJ Day at her school. But her teammates had egged her on for not participating, so for the first time she had chosen to do it. That morning, as she was getting coffee in the workroom, she was unhappy and felt like she'd been forced into doing something she hadn't wanted to. However, by the end of the day, her attitude had been changed. She'd been pleasantly surprised by how excited her kids were to see her dressed up in her PJs. It turned out to have been a fun day, and she was happy to have been a part of the group picture with her coworkers. Dress-up days may appear to have no purpose other than being silly, but they are so much more. Spirit days like this one bring you together, help you connect with your team and your students, and build memories that help to create a strong bond within the walls of the school.

Execute Passion Days

Shiloh Point Elementary came up with an ingenious way for their teachers and administrators to connect their passion with their work and impact their students. Once a quarter, every teacher in the school is assigned a classroom and given an opportunity to share their passion with others. One teacher may be into Cross-Fit, while others' hobbies could be cooking, basketball, knitting, or Scrabble. The point is for one hour, they get to share their passion or hobby with students and teachers alike.

Play Small to Play Big

Play can start immediately. It doesn't have to be a big formal announcement that we are going to incorporate play into our day. Simply switch up a staff meeting. Conduct an icebreaker or play a game. Have people share jokes or tell funny stories. Do something different with the morning announcements. Just switching up the daily routine even a little bit will get things started!

Effectively using play for staff connection and morale is a series of small things. Just get the process started and let it build. Once people feel joy and energy, you will be amazed at how it will build organically. So many memories and joy can be created through the spirit of play. Make your school one of those schools where all teachers want to work.

COMPANION GUIDE ACTIVITY: INSTILLING A PLAYFUL NATURE

Play is one of the most effective tools for keeping relationships exciting. It brings vitality and resilience to relationships as well as healing resentments and divisiveness. While it allows us to feel comfortable and safe with one another, play also builds trust. Trust allows us to open up to be vulnerable and truly maximize the meaning and productivity derived from our relationships.

Organization: What organizational changes or adjustments should be made (new roles or team structures)?

_____

_____

_____

_____

People: What professional development, book studies, and self-paced learning should be added?

_____

_____

_____

_____

Process: What activities can be added or integrated within the current schedule?

_____

_____

_____

_____

Technology and Tools: How can we leverage technology and tools?

_____

_____

_____

_____

8
CHAPTER

THE JOURNEY AND THE PRIZE

MOVING FORWARD WITH COURAGE

There are two main misconceptions in education. The first is that it's all cotton candy and rainbows—an "easy" job. The other is that it's a disaster and there are no solutions. Both of these perspectives are extremely unhealthy and unsustainable.

Paulo Freire is a Brazilian educator and philosopher best known for his influential work, *Pedagogy of Hope: Reliving Pedagogy of the Oppressed*. He has been quoted to have said, "Hope is found between acknowledging our concrete realities and actively working toward the dreams of what is still possible." The genius in this perspective is acknowledging the struggle is real, without losing hope and recognizing the incredible potential we all have as educators.

Education is hard. You will see things that break your heart. You will fail and come up short over and over. You will part ways with people who you care about. You will be criticized unfairly by people who don't know you. You will have to take great leaps of faith when it's hard to see positive outcomes. You will have to trust yourself and your leadership. You have to remind yourself "This too will pass," and that tomorrow will be a better day.

The Stockdale Paradox is named after Admiral Jim Stockdale, who was a United States military officer held captive for eight years during the Vietnam War. Stockdale was tortured more than twenty times by his captors and never had much reason to believe he would survive the prison camp and get to see his wife again.

Stockdale was interviewed by Jim Collins for his book *Good to Great*. When asked about the people who weren't able to survive, Stockdale responded, "The optimists." It seems counterintuitive, but Stockdale explained further. "They were the ones who said, 'We're going to be out by Christmas.' And Christmas would come, and Christmas would go. Then they'd say, 'We're going to be out by Easter.' And Easter would come, and Easter would go. And then Thanksgiving, and then it would be Christmas again. And they died of a broken heart."[25]

The idea of the Stockdale Paradox is that in the face of adversity, one needs to be able to balance optimism with acknowledgment of the reality of the situation. While Stockdale and other survivors remained steadfast in the belief they would be saved, they never failed to fully recognize the harsh realities of their situation. This is how great educators think. They acknowledge the struggle is real, but they never lose sight of the possibilities. They know every student is a beautiful mix of struggle, challenge, and

---

[25] Collins, *Good to Great*, 102–105.

incredible potential. They feel and know the same is true for each of their colleagues.

The dream of education becomes bigger than any moment of challenge. The beauty of your work is this: every little ounce of knowledge or goodness you pour into a student or educator makes the world a better place for everyone. Who knows which student or teacher it will be that day? Who knows who might be in a critical moment when one word, one smile, or one act of confidence will change the course of their life? But great educators know that person is walking the halls today, and today they are going to make a difference in his or her life.

FLAPPING OUR WINGS

Think about the Butterfly Effect. Just like a butterfly flapping its wings in Asia could be the catalyst for a hurricane in the Caribbean, the Butterfly Effect refers to the impact small changes in one situation can have on seemingly separate, different later situations. Everything that happens, good and bad, is the culmination of many small influences. In other words, it's the little things that create the big things and, conversely, the big things are the culmination of a whole bunch of little things.

Now imagine we could get every adult on the team into the right place, where they could be the most authentic and best version of themselves. What if we could all be our best in the moments of greatest need to have the greatest impact? To get there we cannot count on always having a great group of students or families each year. We will never have the perfect team—there will always be challenge and strife. We can't wait around for the government to invoke transformative legislation that might never happen.

The answer resides in an often-overlooked place. The solution must start from the bottom up and from the inside out. Each of us has to be better, but that task is almost impossible if we don't band together. We must build the relationships that foster trust, belonging, and significance for all of us, and for that to happen we need to establish clarity, conflict, belief, nurture, and play within our teams. We must make our schools that place where we can be our authentic best. This can only be done if we work with each other rather than separately from or against one another.

You are the heroes of education. Now embrace your courage and go make your schools *ridiculously amazing!*

9
CHAPTER

HOW TO MAKE YOUR SCHOOL RIDICULOUSLY AMAZING

Through our research and interaction with extraordinary educators, a number of tenets have surfaced consistently in schools with courageous relationships. The key is creating an environment where educators can function and perform at their authentic best. This requires a collective feeling of trust among the team and an individual sense of belonging and significance. To foster this courage, great schools embrace clarity, healthy conflict, nurture, belief, and play among the team. These are the primary practices that create an environment where every educator can thrive, find their authentic power, and impact the students to the maximum extent.

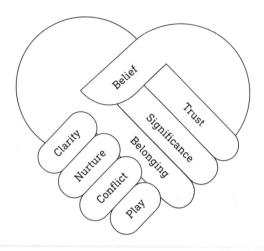

This book and companion guide have been designed to meet every school where they currently are. The key is to start taking action and moving your collective team toward higher levels of courage. Every tiny step that we take to improve the relationships in our school benefits every educator as well as every student in the school. Likewise, schools that maintain high levels of courage always have opportunity for improvement. As we have learned from many of the great educational leaders: you are either moving forward or you are moving backward. The key is to continue to assess and grow each and every year.

Step 1: Assess

A high-level Assessment Tool has been provided that allows you to measure where you stand individually and collectively as an educational team. You will find the assessment questions integrated throughout the chapters are also aggregated into one tool included in the Appendix and accessible at www.7mindsets.com/RAS.

This tool can be taken individually or collectively. If you need assistance managing or facilitating this process, email us at info@7Mindsets.com. A school-wide Assessment is available school-wide that provides a more thorough analysis and guidance on how best to move forward. Both the high-level and detailed assessments act as a resource to take before and after you begin focusing on the critical initiatives that will have the greatest impact on the relationships among the educators.

The charts below provide examples of how an illustrative school might assess itself on the Three Conditions of Courage and the Five Elements. A blank version of both charts is provided in the Assessment Tool in the Appendix. With this, you can begin to understand where the greatest areas of opportunity are for your school to increase its level of courage. The school in the example below would reap the greatest benefit with an initial focus on building trust through fostering belief and healthy conflict.

Illustrative Assessment
(Three Conditions of Courage)

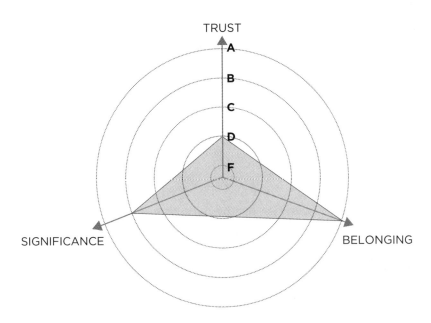

Illustrative Assessment (The Five Elements)

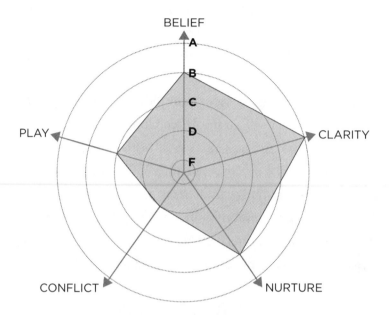

Step 2: Act

The assessment will provide us the ability to focus our efforts in the areas of greatest need and ultimate impact. Once you have clarity of focus, go back and review the different suggestions made in "The Time Is Now" sections of each chapter. These are a collection of the best practices we encountered through our observations and interviews. They can be a source of proven approaches to foster courageous relationships.

Equipped with our suggestions, work as a team to complete the appropriate sections of the Companion Guide. These are designed to be engaging, reflective exercises that allow educators to collaborate and jointly define approaches to maximizing the potential of every member of the team. If you need assistance managing or facilitating this process, email us at info@7Mindsets. com. As a team, develop a series of strategies and approaches that will work for your very unique environment. Critical to this will be setting a timeline in which you can reassess and measure if the efforts are working.

Step 3: Adjust

Transforming relationships is a journey. As you address and grow in some areas, new areas will become the priority. The Assessment Tool will allow you to continue deepening the courage within your team to empower the students you teach. At the appropriate time, re-execute the assessment to see how you are improving and what other areas of focus now need attention. Based on this new data, review our suggestions and revisit the appropriate areas of the Companion Guide. With this new information, develop and execute new initiatives to continue to drive your culture to higher and higher levels.

APPENDIX

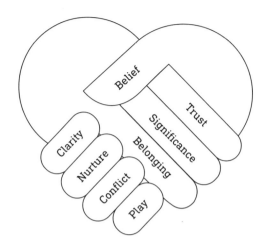

HIGH-LEVEL ASSESSMENT TOOL

Building Trust, Belonging, and Significance through Clarity, Conflict, Belief, Nurture, and Play

Instructions: There are two versions of the Assessment Tool. The first is included in this book and online at www.7mindsets.com/RAS. This high-level tool is designed to allow any team to quickly assess where they stand and where the greatest opportunities lie. The second is a more detailed assessment that provides strategic feedback on exactly how to move forward with optimum impact. That tool can be purchased and used school-wide by emailing info@7mindsets.com.

If you have already read this book, chances are you have already completed some or all of the high-level assessment questions. The following is a complete Assessment Tool that includes every question included in all the chapters.

TRUST

Quiz Question (Circle the grade that applies)					
I trust the members of my team.	A	B	C	D	F
I feel members of the team trust me.	A	B	C	D	F
I feel like I am authentic and genuine at work.	A	B	C	D	F
My overall Trust Score is:	**A**	**B**	**C**	**D**	**F**

SIGNIFICANCE

Quiz Question (Circle the grade that applies)					
I feel like I am very good at the work I do.	A	B	C	D	F
I am recognized appropriately for my contributions.	A	B	C	D	F
Most nights, I go home feeling good about the impact I have at my job.	A	B	C	D	F
My overall Significance Score is:	**A**	**B**	**C**	**D**	**F**

BELONGING

Quiz Question (Circle the grade that applies)					
When I am with my colleagues, I feel like I belong.	A	B	C	D	F
I feel there is a great sense of community among the staff.	A	B	C	D	F
I look forward to the interactions with my team.	A	B	C	D	F
My overall Belonging Score is:	**A**	**B**	**C**	**D**	**F**

Map Your Results

After assessing your team on the Three Conditions of Courage, take some time to plot your results on the chart below. This will provide you with a visual representation of where the greatest opportunities exist for you.

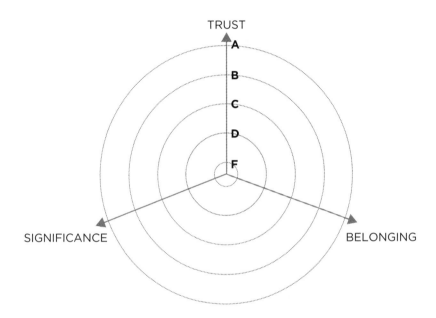

BELIEF

Quiz Question (Circle the grade that applies)	
My colleagues are talented and care deeply about their jobs.	A B C D F
My school is in the process of doing great things for its staff and students.	A B C D F
My colleagues and I celebrate our differences.	A B C D F
We work to include different perspectives in the key decisions we make.	A B C D F
I feel empowered by my colleagues.	A B C D F
My overall Belief Score is:	**A B C D F**

CLARITY

Quiz Question (Circle the grade that applies)

I clearly understand the critical goals and objectives of the school.
A B C D F

I believe in the focus and direction of the school.
A B C D F

I have a clear path for my role that aligns with the school's goals and objectives.
A B C D F

The goals and objectives of the school are effectively communicated and constantly reinforced.
A B C D F

The school's goals are directly aligned with the vision put forth by the district.
A B C D F

My overall Clarity Score is:
A B C D F

NURTURE

Quiz Question (Circle the grade that applies)					
We are supportive and take care of one another.	A	B	C	D	F
I feel respected and appreciated.	A	B	C	D	F
When I am having a bad day, others pick me up.	A	B	C	D	F
I am challenged to grow personally and professionally.	A	B	C	D	F
There are informal and formal support structures to support me and help me develop.	A	B	C	D	F
My overall Nurture Score is:	**A**	**B**	**C**	**D**	**F**

CONFLICT

Quiz Question (Circle the grade that applies)

Our school is good about not gossiping or talking negatively behind each other's backs.	A B C D F
I am comfortable approaching leadership with difficult conversations.	A B C D F
Our team members are skilled at non-defensive communication (e.g., they don't make it personal or take it personally).	A B C D F
I can have a healthy debate with a colleague without feelings getting hurt.	A B C D F
Our team faces our biggest challenges head-on.	A B C D F
My overall Conflict Score is:	**A B C D F**

PLAY

Quiz Question (Circle the grade that applies)					
I am comfortable being myself around my colleagues.	A	B	C	D	F
I have fun at my school.	A	B	C	D	F
Time is created for me to play and connect with colleagues in informal settings.	A	B	C	D	F
I have time to decompress and rejuvenate myself appropriately.	A	B	C	D	F
I enjoy being with my colleagues.	A	B	C	D	F
My overall Play Score is:	**A**	**B**	**C**	**D**	**F**

Map Your Results

After assessing your team on the Five Elements, take some time to plot your results on the chart below. This will provide you with a visual representation of where the greatest opportunities exist for you.

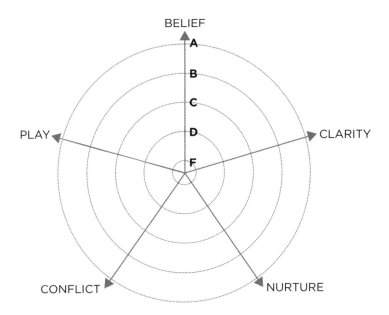

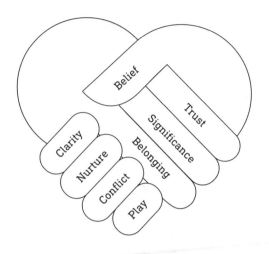

COMPANION GUIDE

Building and Sustaining Courageous Relationships at Your School

Instructions: The Companion Guide is a tool to assist your team to best define initiatives to drive courage throughout your organization. Use the results from the Assessment Tool to inform your use of this Companion Guide as you determine how to move forward in the four critical areas of school transformation:

1. **Organization:** Are new roles, responsibilities, or team structures required?
2. **People:** Is new training or professional development necessary?
3. **Process:** Can new activities and projects be integrated within the schedule?

4. **Technology and Tools:** Will technology or new tools help foster positive growth?

We encourage you to sit down as a team and define what works best within the current environment at your school. Get started today building the courage within your organization. Use the Assessment Tool to periodically review how you are doing and make adjustments.

EXERCISE 1:
BUILDING BELIEF

Belief is the perspective of seeing the higher part of each other. In many ways, belief is the trickiest of the catalysts for courageous relationships, yet it might just be the most powerful. It goes against human nature and generations of conditioning. Our ability to see the higher part of our colleagues and expect greatness is a primary driver of trust in ourselves and those we work with. It also fosters a strong sense of belonging and empowers all team members to feel a sense of contribution and significance.

Organization: What organizational changes or adjustments should be made (new roles or team structures)?

_____

_____

_____

_____

People: What professional development, book studies, and self-paced learning should be added?

_____

_____

_____

_____

Process: What activities can be added or integrated within the current schedule?

_____

_____

_____

_____

Technology and Tools: How can we leverage technology and tools?

_____

_____

_____

_____

EXERCISE 2:
CREATING CLARITY

Clarity requires abundant communication and debate. Creating a shared vision and finding a common ground takes time, determination, and persistence. You must be intentional about defining your "win." Remember that sustaining clarity is a thousand acts of courage every single day.

Organization: What organizational changes or adjustments should be made (new roles or team structures)?

_____

_____

_____

_____

People: What professional development, book studies, and self-paced learning should be added?

_____

_____

_____

_____

Process: What activities can be added or integrated within the current schedule?

_____

_____

_____

_____

Technology and Tools: How can we leverage technology and tools?

_____

_____

_____

_____

EXERCISE 3:
FOSTERING NURTURE

A nurturing environment has two critical components. First, it lets everyone know that they are supported, that we have their backs. Second, it firmly challenges each of us to foster individual and collective growth, knowing that one person's growth improves us all. It requires that we see ourselves as part of the collective whole, that we have a role in everything that happens in the school, and that when one person wins, we all win.

Organization: What organizational changes or adjustments should be made (new roles or team structures)?

_____

_____

_____

_____

People: What professional development, book studies, and self-paced learning should be added?

_____

_____

_____

_____

Process: What activities can be added or integrated within the current schedule?

_____

_____

_____

_____

Technology and Tools: How can we leverage technology and tools?

_____

_____

_____

_____

EXERCISE 4:
BUILDING CONSTRUCTIVE CONFLICT

Healthy conflict is an essential part of the growth process. It takes courage to allow conflicts to build relationships, rather than tear them down. Knowing how you handle conflict is also important in dealing with issues when they come up. When we address conflict openly and when we can move forward constructively, it becomes a catalyst for not only trust but creativity, innovation, and—ultimately—sustained excellence.

Organization: What organizational changes or adjustments should be made (new roles or team structures)?

People: What professional development, book studies, and self-paced learning should be added?

Process: What activities can be added or integrated within the current schedule?

_____

_____

_____

_____

Technology and Tools: How can we leverage technology and tools?

_____

_____

_____

_____

EXERCISE 5:
INSTILLING A PLAYFUL NATURE

Play is one of the most effective tools for keeping relationships exciting. It brings vitality and resilience to relationships as well as healing resentments and divisiveness. While it allows us to feel comfortable and safe with one another, play also builds trust. Trust allows us to open up to be vulnerable and truly maximize the meaning and productivity derived from our relationships.

Organization: What organizational changes or adjustments should be made (new roles or team structures)?

_____

_____

_____

_____

People: What professional development, book studies, and self-paced learning should be added?

_____

_____

_____

_____

Process: What activities can be added or integrated within the current schedule?

_____

_____

_____

_____

Technology and Tools: How can we leverage technology and tools?

_____

_____

_____

_____

ACKNOWLEDGMENTS

This book could not have been written without the critical support of some key individuals along the way. We are so thankful to have had them on this journey with us.

Adelma Brown—For being so real, so comfortable in your own skin, and so courageous and powerful with your voice. You are a role model for young women everywhere.

Charles Bonner—For modeling the way for so many. Your quiet influence has left an imprint on so many students, your humble leadership has allowed so many teachers to fill empowered in their work, and your unconditional love has allowed me to become who I am today.

Peggy Bonner—For your spirit and commitment to family. For answering the call every time we needed Gran! I could not do it all without you.

Chelsea Buchanan—For being a light along the path. For bringing goodness, love, and positive energy to everything you do. For making us better and more authentic than we could have ever been without you.

Juan Casimiro (Papi)—We would not be here without you. It was your energy and your relationships that were leveraged to get it all started. Your DNA will forever be deeply a part of all we do.

Ellen Cohan—For mentoring so many teachers and administrators. The world is a much better place because you are in it.

Vince Coyner—For being there in the beginning. Your creativity was always ahead of us but many times you led the way for us.

Mahmoud Dahy—You were the missing piece. Your ability to create something so powerful out of nothing is a gift to us and to this world. Keep working your beautiful magic.

Dr. Mimi Gamel—You were there with us in the beginning and we pray you will be with us in the end. It was divine intervention that we crossed paths.

Beth Hench—For your fierce determination to make the world a better place and your crazy smart thinking.

Dr. Kimothy Jarrett—For being crazy enough to believe in us in the beginning. Your confidence in us was a catalyst for all we have done.

Kirk Jones—For your spirit, drive, and friendship. Your out-of-the-box thinking is going to change the world.

Caroline King—For bringing a spirit of play and joy but also of discipline and toughness. It is the little things you do that truly are the big things.

Chris Koke—For being the spark, the light of enthusiasm that allowed us to overcome the early challenges. For doing whatever was needed, whenever it was needed for the purpose of helping others.

Lupita Knittel—For bringing new magic to the 7 Mindsets. For making us more of what we wanted to be, and for teaching us that all who wander are truly not lost.

Barb Mamoine—For your energy. You give us courage and confidence to do what we have never done and to get to places we could have only once dreamed of.

Duane Moyer—For your courage to act, to push the world around just a little so we could truly understand and become better.

Lilly Posada-Waller—For being my rock. For the sacrifices you make and the joy you find in my accomplishments. I only wish everyone could have what you give me. The world would be such a better place.

Gabi Perez—For helping us to express ourselves and share our voices with the world. The greatest of words are meaningless if they are never heard.

Kyle Porter—For helping us see the walls outside of education and for all the amazing conversations that lead to great ideas.

Chris Post—For your moxy and your ability to jump in, take action, and make progress. For your patience and vision to see the possibility and play the long game that will be the key to victory in the end.

Mary Claire Powell—For your unwavering dedication to growing as a leader. For your forward thinking and passionate energy to education.

Mitch Schlimer—For being there in the beginning when it was just an idea. For talking us off the ledge and keeping us focused on the dream. Your contributions have been great and lasting.

Nashid Sharrief—For showing us that there are no bad children, only children making bad decisions. Through your heart, we saw connections that transformed lives. You are an inspiration.

Scott Shickler—For the platform to fulfill our dreams. For the courage to be bold and keep going when most would stop. For teaching us that greatness is the journey and the struggle is much more than the prize.

Jeff Smith—For being an incredibly strong man of faith who is a true shepherd for others. My life is *awesmazingly* blessed with you by my side.

Matt Smith—For freeing the way for us to express our best selves. For making us great in all the areas that allow everyone to be great.

Julie Spierto—For your energy, your kindness and your enthusiasm. You bring nothing but positivity to everything we do and we are blessed you have joined our journey.

Adam Stern—For being there in the beginning. For stepping up and solving problems when they needed to be solved. Your contributions will never be forgotten.

Krista Stippich—For your discipline, focus, and determination. For your unwavering commitment, not to perfection, but to the very best we are capable of.

Jennifer Swaim—For every adventure we've been on. For every tough convo we'd prepared for together. For being by my side, having my back, and finishing my sentences! This adventure would not have been possible without you.

Sarah Von Esh—For being so passionate about kids but also so humble. You are a beautiful soul!

Deedee Westbrook—We knew of your greatness the moment we met. For being a truly extraordinary principal and inspiration to the 7 Mindsets.

Mitch Young—Thank you for being my accountability partner, for telling me like it is and for your fierce leadership. We are blessed to have you leading the way.

Mashburn Elementary—For your willingness to try new things, trust before belief, and for your dedication to children. For your strong commitment to make today RIDICULOUSLY amazing for students, families, and each other.

Brookwood Elementary—For your determination and drive to do what's best for kids. For your willingness to open up, get funky, and to Go Be Awesome!

KEY CONTRIBUTORS

This book is the culmination of ten years of research working directly with schools around the country. The following people inspired us and have provided key insights that helped us form the key conclusions of this book.

Allen, Patti Ann	Assistant Principal	Brookwood Elementary School
Barlow Jr., Chuck	Co-founder	SOSSI—Saving our Sons and Sisters International
Barlow, Patrice	Co-founder	SOSSI—Saving our Sons and Sisters International
Barnes, Angela	Elementary Teacher	Brookwood Elementary School
Bearden, Dr. Jeff	Superintendent	Forsyth County Schools
Belleza, Rouel	Supervisor, Student Services	Cherokee County School District
Berger, Sarah	Teacher	Mashburn Elementary School
Bonner, Charles	Retired Principal	Valdosta City School District
Bryant, Lori	Counselor	Forsyth County Schools
Buchanan, Chelsea	Director of Education	7 Mindsets
Burns, Gina	Assistant Principal	Forsyth County Schools
Casimiro, Juan	President	Biznovator

Clack, Andrea	Academic Coach	Mashburn Elementary School
Cohan, Ellen	Educational Leadership Coach	Ellen Cohan Consulting
Cook, Keri	Special Education Teacher	Forsyth County Schools
Culpepper, Dave	Retired Principal	Forsyth County Schools
Cunningham, Karon	Principal	Franklin Middle School
Cutrer, Emily	Teacher	Forsyth County Schools
Dahy, Mahmoud	Director of Product Development	7 Mindsets
Daniel, Mike	Co-Founder	Atlas Ministries
Davis, Barron	Superintendent	Richland School District Two
Day, Paul	Assistant Principal	Valdosta City School District
Degliumberto, Alyssa	Principal	Matt Elementary
Farlow, April	Consultant and Motivational Speaker	Dale Carnegie
Finstad, Paul	Executive Director	YMCA of Cass and Clay Counties
Fort, Carol	Special Education Teacher	Forsyth County Schools
Franks, Jan	Principal	West Point Elementary School
Gamel, Dr. Mimi	Assistant Principal and Researcher	Autrey Mill Middle School
Gibbs, Jennifer	Guidance Counselor	St. Pius X High School
Glasser, Howard	Creator	Nurtured Heart Approach
Greer, Yolanda	Principal	Vista Peak Exploratory School
Hench, Beth	Principal	Ayersville Elementary School
Hershey, Derrick	Principal	Sawnee Elementary School
Hodgson, Amy	Superintendent	Dansville School District
Holdsworth, Julie	Principal	Mesquite Elementary School
Hollowel, Jean	Executive Director	Children's Success Foundation
Holton Arnol, Tammy	President	Children's Success Foundation

ACKNOWLEDGMENTS

Humeniuk, Jaclyn	Teacher	Brookwood Elementary
Jarrett, Kimothy	Principal	Crabapple Middle School
Johnson, Jeannie	Teacher	South Forsyth High School
Johnson, Rebecca	Teaching and Learning	Forsyth County Schools
Jones, Kirk	Principal	Ayersville Middle School
Laskey, Wendy	Teacher	Lowndes County Schools
Lewis, Valerie	Assistant Principal	Discovery Genesis Center
Lochbaum, Kim	Instructional Support Specialist	Forsyth County Schools
Lyons, Sam	Counselor	Forsyth County Schools
Martinez, Joe	Technology Education Teacher	Monte Vista School
McCormick, Jane	Teacher	Forsyth County Schools
Miller, Steve	Principal	Otwell Middle School
Moon, Cori	Singer/Parent	Forsyth County Schools
Morris, Rebecca	Teacher	Shiloh Point Elementary
Murdock, Jaime	Assistant Principal	Lee County Primary School
Murrieta, Jennifer	Principal	Casa Grande Elementary School
Norton, Candy	Retired HR Director	Forsyth County Schools
Paluzzi, Mo	Instructional Technology Specialist	Forsyth County Schools
Perryman, Beth	Teacher	Chattahoochee Elementary School
Philmon, Julia	Teacher	Forsyth County Schools
Pijanowski, Lissa	Educational Consultant	International Center for Leadership in Education, Inc.
Porter, Kyle	Owner	The DoJo
Post, Claire	Teacher	Settles Bridge Elementary School
Powell, Mary Claire	Instructional Coach	Forsyth County Schools
Rice, Pat	Speech/Language Pathologist	Forsyth County Schools
Rosenbluth, Nicky	Executive Director of Talent and Leadership Development	YMCA of Metro Atlanta

Saladin, Dr. Rosanna	Assistant Director, Community Partnerships	Charlotte-Mecklenburg Schools
Sharrief, Nashid	Founder	My Higher Self Consulting
Shariott, Caroline	Counselor	Forsyth County Schools
Shell, April	Principal	Summit Parkway Middle School
Smith, Debbie	Director of Student Support Services	Forsyth County Schools
Spierto, Julie	High School Math Teacher	South Forsyth High School
Stippich, Krista	Director of Account Management	7 Mindsets
Stovall, Connie	Principal	Dawson County Jr. High
Swaim, Jennifer	Assistant Principal	Mashburn Elementary School
Tinsley, Sandy	Principal	South Forsyth Middle School
Traynor, Pat	Executive Director	Dakota Medical Foundation
Vella, Barbara	Principal	Chattahoochee Elementary School
Victor Robertson, Mandi	Educational Consultant, Writer, Teacher	Durham School of the Arts
Von Esh, Sarah	Principal	Settles Bridge Elementary School
Wall, Sasha	Director of Product Management	K12 Inc.
Wallace, Traci	Teacher/Coach	Mashburn Elementary School
Watts, Erin	Teacher	Brookwood Elementary School
Weber, Michelle	Principal	Liberty Middle School
Westwood, Deedee	Principal	Mid-Carolina Middle School
White, Sara	Special Education Teacher	Forsyth County Schools
Wildes, Anna	Teacher	Coal Mountain Elementary School
Winters, Colleen	Teacher	Park Elementary
Young, Mitch	Principal	Forsyth Central High School

RESOURCES

This book is the culmination of three decades of working with youth, studying great educators, and learning from great authors and thought leaders. We wanted to recognize the great works that formed a big part of the philosophy, thinking, and conclusions of this book. Below is a list of books that we found inspirational and would recommend to anyone for their own personal and professional development.

Bench, Doug. *Revolutionize Your Brain!* Florida: Doug Bench Enterprises, 2009.

Bolles, Richard N. and Carol Christen with Jean M. Blomquist. *What Color is Your Parachute? For Teens: Discovering Yourself, Defining Your Future.* Berkeley, CA: Ten Speed Press, 2010.

Brodie, Richard. *Virus of the Mind: The New Science of the Meme.* Carlsbad, CA: Hay House, 2009.

Brown, Brené. *Daring Greatly: How the Courage to Be Vulnerable Transforms the Way We Live, Love, Parent, and Lead.* New York: Gotham Books, 2012.

Brown, Brené. *The Power of Vulnerability: Teachings on Authenticity, Connection, and Courage.* Read by Brené Brown. Sounds True, 2012. Audiobook.

Brown, Brené. *I Thought It Was Just Me (But It Isn't): Making the Journey from "What Will People Think?" to "I Am Enough."* New York: Avery, 2007.

Brown, Stuart L. *Play: How It Shapes the Brain, Opens the Imagination, and Invigorates the Soul.* New York: Avery, 2009.

Buckingham, Marcus and Donald O. Clifton. *Now, Discover Your Strengths.* New York: Free Press, 2001.

Canfield, Jack. *The Success Principles: How to Get from Where You Are to Where You Want to Be.* New York: William Morrow, 2015.

Carnegie, Dale. *How to Win Friends and Influence People.* New York: Simon & Schuster, 1937.

Collins, Jim. *Good to Great: Why Some Companies Make the Leap … and Others Don't.* New York: HarperBusiness, 2001.

Colvin, Geoffrey. *Talent is Overrated: What Really Separates World-Class Performers from Everybody Else.* New York: Portfolio, 2018.

Connors, Neila A. *If You Don't Feed the Teachers, They Eat the Students!: Guide to Success for Administrators and Teachers.* Nashville: Incentive Publications, 2000.

Dalai Lama. *The Art of Happiness: A Handbook for Living.* 10th anniversary ed. New York: Riverhead Books, 2009.

DeLuca, Fred with John P. Hayes. *Start Small, Finish Big: Fifteen Key Lessons to Start—and Run—Your Own Business.* New York: Warner Books, 2000.

Demartini, John. *The Gratitude Effect.* Burman Books Media Corp, 2007.

Dweck, Carol. *Mindset: The New Psychology of Success.* New York: Random House, 2016.

Forstater, Mark. *The Spiritual Teachings of Marcus Aurelius.* New York: HarperCollins, 2000.

Frankl, Viktor E. *Man's Search for Meaning.* Boston: Beacon Press, 2017.

Gardner, Howard. *Frames of Mind: The Theory of Multiple Intelligences.* New York: Basic Books, 2011.

Gelb, Michael J. *How to Think Like Leonardo da Vinci: Seven Steps to Genius Every Day.* New York: Delacorte Press, 1998.

Gladwell, Malcom. *Outliers: The Story of Success.* New York: Little, Brown and Co., 2008.

Gordon, Jon. *The Energy Bus: 10 Rules to Fuel Your Life, Work, and Team with Positive Energy.* Hoboken, NJ: John Wiley & Sons, 2007.

Hardy, Darren. *The Compound Effect: Multiplying Your Success One Simple Step at a Time.* Lake Dallas, TX: Success Books, 2010.

Harrell, Keith. *Attitude is Everything: 10 Life-Changing Steps to Turning Attitude Into Action.* Revised edition. New York: HarperBusiness, 2005.

Hawkins, David R. *Power vs. Force: The Hidden Determinants of Human Behavior.* Carlsbad, CA: Hay House, Inc., 2012.

Helmstetter, Shad. *The Self-Talk Solution.* New York: W. Morrow, 1987.

Hill, Napoleon and W. Clement Stone. *Success Through a Positive Mental Attitude.* New York: Ishi Press International, 2013.

Holiday, Ryan. *Ego is the Enemy.* New York: Portfolio, 2016.

Jolley, Willie. *It Only Takes a Minute to Change Your Life.* Dubuque, IA: Kendall/Hunt Pub. Co., 1994.

Kimbro, Dennis. *What Makes the Great Great: Strategies for Extraordinary Achievement.* New York: Doubleday, 1997.

Koch, Charles G. *The Science of Success: How Market-Based Management Built the World's Largest Private Company.* Hoboken, NJ: Wiley, 2007.

Langer, Ellen J. *Mindfulness*. 25th anniversary ed. Boston: De Capo Press, 2014.

Maxwell, John. *Talent is Never Enough: Discover the Choices that Will Take You Beyond Your Talent*. Nashville, TN: Thomas Nelson, 2007.

Maxwell, John. *The 21 Irrefutable Laws of Leadership Workbook: Follow Them and People Will Follow You*. Nashville, TN: Thomas Nelson, 2007.

May, Matthew E. *In Pursuit of Elegance: Why the Best Ideas Have Something Missing*. New York: Broadway Books, 2010.

McGovern, George. *Abraham Lincoln*. New York: Times Books/ Henry Holt and Co., 2009.

Millman, Dan. *Way of the Peaceful Warrior: A Book That Changes Lives*. Tiburon, CA: H.J. Kramer, 2006.

Peale, Norman Vincent. *The Power of Positive Thinking*. New York: Prentice-Hall, 1952.

Peck, M. Scott. *The Road Less Traveled: A New Psychology of Love, Traditional Values, and Spiritual Growth*. New York: Simon & Schuster, 2002.

Pink, Daniel. *Drive: The Surprising Truth About What Motivates Us*. New York: Riverhead Books, 2009.

Pink, Daniel. *A Whole New Mind: Why Right-Brainers Will Rule the Future*. New York: Riverhead Books, 2006.

Pinker, Steven. *The Stuff of Thought: Language as a Window into Human Nature*. New York: Viking, 2007.

Redfield, James. *The Celestine Prophecy: An Adventure*. New edition. New York: Grand Central Publishing, 2018.

Robbins, Tony. *Awaken the Giant Within: How to Take Immediate Control of Your Mental, Emotional, Physical, and Financial Destiny!* New York: Simon & Schuster, 1992.

Robbins, Tony. *Unlimited Power: The New Science of Personal Achievement.* New York: Simon & Schuster, 1997.

Robbins, Mike. *Be Yourself, Everyone Else is Already Taken: Transform Your Life with the Power of Authenticity.* San Francisco: Jossey-Bass, 2009.

Robinson, Ken. *The Element: How Finding Your Passion Changes Everything.* New York: Viking, 2009.

Ruiz, Miguel. *The Four Agreements: A Practical Guide to Personal Freedom.* San Rafael, CA: Amber-Allen Publishing, 1997.

Scroggins, Clay. *How to Lead When You're Not in Charge: Leveraging Influence When You Lack Authority.* Grand Rapids, MI: Zondervan, 2017.

Seligman, Martin E. P. *Authentic Happiness: Using the New Positive Psychology to Realize Your Potential for Deep Fulfillment.* Free Press, 2002.

Seligman, Martin E. P. *Learned Optimism: How to Change Your Mind and Your Life.* New York: Vintage Books 2006.

Singer, Michael A. *The Surrender Experiment: My Journey Into Life's Perfection.* New York: Harmony Books, 2015.

Shinn, Florence Scovel. *The Game of Life and How to Play It.* 2nd edition. Carlsbad, CA: Hay House, 2016.

Stanley, Andy. *The Next Generation Leader: 5 Essentials for Those Who Will Shape the Future.* Sisters, OR: Multnomah Books, 2003.

Stanley, Andy. *Making Vision Stick.* Grand Rapids, MI: Zondervan, 2007.

Stone, W. Clement. *Believe and Achieve: W. Clement Stone's 17 Principles of Success.* Rev. edition. Napoleon Hill Foundation: 2002.

Tracy, Brian. *Maximum Achievement: The Proven System of Strategies and Skills That Will Unlock Your Hidden Powers to Succeed.* New York: Simon & Schuster, 1993.

Tzu, Lao. *The Tao Te Ching: A New English Version*. Translated by Stephen Mitchell. New York: Harper Perennial Modern Classics, 2006.

Warren, Rick. *The Purpose Driven Life: What on Earth Am I Here For?* Grand Rapids, MI: Zondervan, 2012.

Wiseman, Liz. *Multipliers: How the Best Leaders Make Everyone Smarter*. Revised and updated edition. New York: Harper-Business, 2017.

Young, Steve. *Great Failures of the Extremely Successful: Mistakes, Adversity, Failure, and Other Steppingstones to Success*. Los Angeles: Tallfellow Press, 2002.

REFERENCES

Block, Peter. *The Empowered Manager: Positive Political Skills at Work.* San Francisco: Jossey-Bass, 1987.

Brown, Stuart L. *Play: How It Shapes the Brain, Opens the Imagination, and Invigorates the Soul.* Read by Michael Hinton. Tantor Audio, 2017.

Chappel, Michelle Millis. "Scientists Find 15 Amazing Benefits of Listening to Music," Lifehack. June 27, 2019. https://www.lifehack.org/317747/scientists-find-15-amazing-benefits-listening-music

Collins, Jim. *Good to Great: Why Some Companies Make the Leap... And Others Don't.* New York: HarperBusiness.

Connors, Neila A. *If You Don't Feed the Teachers, They Eat the Students!: Guide to Success for Administrators and Teachers.* Nashville, TN: Incentive Publications, 2000.

Csikszentmihalyi, Mihaly. *Creativity: Flow and the Psychology of Discovery and Invention.* New York: HarperPerennial, 1997.

Enayati, Amanda. "The Importance of Belonging." Special to CNN, June 1, 2012.

Ginwright, Shawn. "Hope & Healing Keynote." Science of Hope Conference, Foundation for Healthy Generations, Seattle, WA: April 2016.

Goldring, Rebecca, Soheyla Taie, and Minsun Riddles. "Teacher Attrition and Mobility: Results From the 2012–13 Teacher Follow-up Survey," National Center for Education Statistics, September 4, 2014: 3, 6. https://nces.ed.gov/pubs2014/2014077.pdf

Greenberg, M.T., J.L. Brown, and R.M. Abenavoli. "Teacher Stress and Health: Effects on Teachers, Students, and Schools," Edna Bennett Pierce Prevention Research Center, Pennsylvania State University, September 2016. http://prevention.psu.edu/uploads/files/rwjf430428.pdf

Hall, Karyn. "Create a Sense of Belonging." *Psychology Today*, March 24, 2014. https://www.psychologytoday.com/us/blog/pieces-mind/201403/create-sense-belonging

Isaacson, Walter. *Steve Jobs.* New York: Simon & Schuster, 2011.

Lencioni, Patrick. *Overcoming the Five Dysfunctions of a Team: A Field Guide for Leaders, Managers, and Facilitators.* San Francisco: Jossey-Bass, 2005.

National Center for Education Statistics. "Teacher Turnover: Stayers, Movers, and Leavers." November 2015. https://nces.ed.gov/programs/coe/indicator_slc.asp

Nelson, Jane, Lynn Lott, and H. Stephen Glenn, *Positive Discipline in the Classroom: Developing Mutual Respect, Cooperation, and Responsibility in Your Classroom.* Read by Jane Nelson. Cincinnati, OH: Empowering People, Inc., 2017.

Nemo, John. "What a NASA Janitor Can Teach Us About Living a Bigger Life." *The Business Journals.* December 23, 2014. https://www.bizjournals.com/bizjournals/how-to/growth-strategies/2014/12/what-a-nasa-janitor-can-teach-us.html

Organisation for Economic Co-operation and Development. "Teachers Love Their Job But Feel Undervalued, Unsupported and Unrecognized, Says OECD." Last modified June 25, 2014. https://www.oecd.org/newsroom/teachers-love-their-job-but-feel-undervalued-unsupported-and-unrecognised.htm

Redding, Christopher and Gary T. Henry. "Leaving School Early: An Examination of Novice Teachers' Within- and End-of-Year Turnover." *American Educational Research Journal*, August 12, 2018. https://doi.org/10.3102/0002831218790542

Seligman, Martin E.P. and Tracy A. Steen. "Positive Psychology Progress Empirical Validation of Interventions." *Journal of the Norwegian Psychological Association* 42, 2005: 879–880. https://pdfs.semanticscholar.org/e83e/c1739d233acebe78d5df0b56b2c6f6f42691.pdf

Shulman, Lee S. *The Wisdom of Practice: Essays on Teaching, Learning, and Learning to Teach.* San Francisco: Jossey Bass, 2004.

Sinek, Simon. *Start with Why: How Great Leaders Inspire Everyone to Take Action.* New York, Penguin Audio, 2017. Audiobook, track 15.

Tyng, Chai M. et al. "The Influences of Emotion on Learning and Memory." *Frontiers in Psychology* 8, no. 1454, (2017). https://doi.org/10.3389/fpsyg.2017.01454

University of Oslo. "The Fold-Processing of Bog Iron." September 30, 2017, https://www.khm.uio.no/english/research/projects/langeid/project/iron-steel/folding/

Visible Learning. "Collective Teacher Efficacy (CTE) According to John Hattie." September 17, 2019. https://visible-learning.org/2018/03/collective-teacher-efficacy-hattie/

ABOUT THE AUTHORS

Tracey Smith works as a principal with Forsyth County Schools in Cumming, Georgia. Her passion for reaching and teaching the whole child led to a friendship with the 7 Mindsets in 2012, when she oversaw the development of an elementary curriculum to address the growing need of social-emotional learning. She is fiercely determined to create environments for teachers and students that change their lives and *make every day ridiculously amazing*.

Tracey has spent the last twenty-two years in education, and fourteen of those have been in administration. She follows the footsteps of her dad, who was a high school administrator in south Georgia. She grew up walking the halls and learning about leading from his amazing example.

Tracey enjoys traveling to present and share lessons learned and teacher empowerment. She believes that we are here to support and grow one another. We are all in this together. Tracey lives in Cumming with her husband and two children, Jordan and Josie. You can find Tracey on Twitter @TBSmith01.

Jeff Waller is a thought leader in social and emotional learning, personal achievement, and youth empowerment. He is the co-author of *The 7 Mindsets to Live Your Ultimate Life*. He is the co-founder of the 7 Mindsets company, a social and emotional learning solution provider serving millions of students and educators in over thirty-seven states.

Jeff has spent the last fifteen years observing hundreds of schools and thousands of classrooms. He has interviewed over 100 of the most successful administrators and teachers in the country. Through this work he has co-authored two books and co-developed the revolutionary 7 Mindsets program that delivers curriculum and professional development to schools and classrooms from kindergarten to twelfth grade.

A motivational speaker, Jeff is also the co-founder of the Magic Wand Foundation, an organization dedicated to empowering youth to live their dreams and make a positive impact on the world. Jeff is also co-creator of the Ultimate Life Summit, a blended empowerment event that combines dynamic live seminars with existing and emerging tools to promote youth empowerment.

He has dedicated the last two decades to learning and understanding the critical elements that define high achievers. Jeff lives in Roswell, Georgia with his wife and three children. You can find Jeff on Twitter @JeffMWaller.

ABOUT 7 MINDSETS

Make Your School Ridiculously Amazing with the 7 Mindsets!

We can't solve the problems we face at the same level of thinking that created them.
– Albert Einstein

After years of working with hundreds of thousands of students and educators, and conducting extensive research on personal achievement, success, and fulfillment, Jeff Waller and Scott Shickler co-created the 7 Mindsets, an organization that delivers social-emotional learning programs to K–12 schools and youth organizations.

Tracey Smith and many of the educators who share their stories in *Ridiculously Amazing Schools* are among the tens of thousands of educators around the country who've seen vast improvements in their schools' cultures and communities through the 7 Mindsets.

7 Mindsets' methodology empowers students and educators to uncover their potential, take pride in their uniqueness, and put their skills and interests to work building better futures for themselves and the world around them.

If you're looking for resources to help transform your school's culture in the ways laid out in *Ridiculously Amazing Schools*, contact 7 Mindsets to learn more.

Tracey Smith and Jeff Waller are also available to deliver keynote presentations and professional development workshops. For more information, please contact:

7 Mindsets
info@7mindsets.com
www.7mindsets.com
(678) 878-3144

ALSO AVAILABLE BY THE AUTHOR

This book is also available in Spanish. For Bulk Orders and Education Discounts, please contact the 7 Mindsets Company at:

info@7mindsets.com
www.7mindsets.com
(678) 878-3144